# Little Girl Lost

## BY THE SAME AUTHOR

# CASEY WATSON

THE MILLION COPY BESTSELLING AUTHOR

## Little Girl Lost

Amelie just wants a
home she feels safe in...

HARPER
element

This book is a work of non-fiction based on the author's experiences.
In order to protect privacy, names, identifying characteristics,
dialogue and details have been changed or reconstructed.

HarperElement
An imprint of HarperCollins*Publishers*
1 London Bridge Street
London SE1 9GF

www.harpercollins.co.uk

HarperCollins*Publishers*
Macken House, 39/40 Mayor Street Upper
Dublin 1, D01 C9W8, Ireland

First published by HarperElement 2024

3 5 7 9 10 8 6 4

© Casey Watson 2024

Casey Watson asserts the moral right to
be identified as the author of this work

A catalogue record of this book is
available from the British Library

PB ISBN 9780008641665
EB ISBN 9780008641672

Printed and bound in the UK using 100%
renewable electricity at CPI Group (UK) Ltd

All rights reserved. No part of this publication may be
reproduced, stored in a retrieval system, or transmitted,
in any form or by any means, electronic, mechanical,
photocopying, recording or otherwise, without the
prior written permission of the publishers.

MIX
Paper | Supporting
responsible forestry
FSC™ C007454

This book contains FSC™ certified paper and other controlled
sources to ensure responsible forest management.

For more information visit: www.harpercollins.co.uk/green

# Dedication

I want to dedicate this to all those who made it through those strange times during the worldwide pandemic. Especially to those who lost loved ones and suffered the heartbreak that went along with it. But also to those who, like me, muddled through, and somehow got to grips with home schooling and being confined to our homes for all that time. In a strange way, it was a time for learning about ourselves too. It was as if the world slowed down and allowed us to step off for a while and get back to basics, and things such as fast food became unnecessary. We began preparing meals from scratch again, and baking fresh bread and cakes. We took to art and music and poetry. In all, I believe that when the world stood still for that moment in history, we woke up and learned how to live.

RIP to all our lost loved ones.

# Acknowledgements

As ever, I have some important people to thank: my fabulous agent, Andrew Lownie, and the incredible team at HarperCollins, my publishing family, whose skill and expertise continue to bring these stories to you so brilliantly.

I must also give thanks to my friend and partner-in-writing-crime, Lynne Barrett-Lee. We've become such a team now that we can almost finish one another's sentences. And often do … when we're not busy writing, that is.

Once again, I cannot pass up the opportunity to thank my amazing family and friends, who continue to keep me sane, and support me in myriad ways. I simply could not do what I do without you.

Finally, I'd once again like to acknowledge all of you, my lovely readers. Your kind reviews really are all the encouragement I need to keep sharing stories of these so often forgotten children. You are the best. I send my love to you all.

# Chapter 1

## April

My dreams, just lately, had been laced with worry. Were full of stress and anxiety and those horrible fight-or-flight situations. Except I could never do either because I had that horrible sleep-paralysis thing where, however awful the thing that I needed to run from or wrestle with, I'd be totally rooted to the spot.

This was, I presumed, all just part of my 'new normal', as everyone had taken to calling it. The new normal of a global pandemic. (Though what's normal, frankly, about a global pandemic?) Yet that was where we were, just a few weeks into the horror that was Covid, and were already used to the prime minister appearing on our TV screens on a daily basis, standing behind his lectern in that oak-panelled office, looking crumpled and unkempt, and reeling off grim statistics and death tolls. It was horrible, and I for one was glad about the fact that Mike had been laid off and put on 'furlough' (another new word for us, just as it probably was for many), so was safe at home with me.

I knew it was bad for people not on furlough who were unable to go into work and do their jobs, and I worried just as much as the next person about how my extended family were going to cope financially. But, if I'm being honest, I was glad that Mike's was one of the many thousands of businesses forced to shut up shop for the duration because the days would have been very long and lonely, and very, very boring, if I was stuck at home alone, separated from my loved ones, and with just that meagre single 'exercise' hour allowed. The world was in chaos, and I needed my sidekick to be with me, not least to be his usual calm, pragmatic self, and to remind me that the situation couldn't last forever, and reassure me that a vaccine could and would soon be found.

Still, one thing Mike couldn't do was intervene in my dreams, which were mostly of dystopian futures and zombie apocalypses, so perhaps it was a blessing that my mobile rang when it did, because it called a halt to a particularly scary one.

Startled awake, I checked the time before answering, to find that it was 1.30 a.m., and I could see from the screen that it was most likely the Emergency Duty Team (EDT) ringing. At least I assumed it was, because theirs was the only No Caller ID number that ever rang at this time of the morning. I did have the EDT number stored in my phone but, out of hours, all the duty staff used their own work mobiles, so, of course, their numbers never came up. As I padded out of the bedroom onto the landing, so as not to wake Mike, I wondered what the protocol was going to be now about taking in any new children. We'd not long said goodbye to our last child (though in Ethan's case it was likely to be more of an *au revoir*, as we knew his dad well) and with no new child on the horizon because we'd already decided to take a few weeks off, just pre-pandemic, I wasn't completely up to speed. We'd all had emails about mask-wearing, ways of mitigating risks of infection, and so on, and had been reassured that social services and fostering agencies would be operating as normally as possible. With no child of our own in, however, and so much else going on (and then some!) I'd only really skim-read the stuff I'd been sent. If they wanted us to take someone now, there would presumably be some adjustments and complications to deal with. Still, it wasn't altogether unwelcome to hear from them, even if it was in the small hours. It wasn't as if we had anything else to do, was it?

It was a man. 'Oh, Mrs Watson!' he exclaimed when I answered, as if my answering the phone was the best thing that had happened to him all night. Perhaps it was. 'Thank *goodness* you picked up. This is Ant Weaver from EDT. We have a grave and ongoing situation here and desperately need a bed for a child as soon as possible. As in tonight.'

'Right,' I said, still trying to wake myself up properly. 'What's the situation?'

'It's a six-year-old. A little girl, rescued from a house fire a couple of hours ago, and we need somewhere to place her asap. Though we don't know for how long at this stage, I'm afraid.'

My heart sank, immediately leaping to the worst-case conclusion; that they needed a bed for her because the rest of her family had died in the fire.

'Oh, the poor mite,' I said, braced for the worst kind of news. 'What's happened to her parents?'

'Parent singular,' Ant answered. 'No father around, at least as far as we know, and the mother should be fine. She's been taken to hospital, as she does have some injuries – mainly from smoke inhalation, I believe – but paramedics say it's not life-threatening.'

'Oh, thank goodness for small mercies,' I said, inadvertently quoting my mother, 'and I'm guessing you've been unable to contact any family members due to the time of night?'

'That's another thing,' Ant said. 'It was a next-door neighbour who alerted the emergency services, and, according to them, in all the time the family have lived there, there haven't been any other family members in the picture. Not as far as they know, anyway. They've also hinted that the mother has some mental health issues, but right now, that's all we know, because the neighbour didn't want to speak out of turn, obviously. Anyway, I see on the system that you don't have any other children in at the minute so, given the circumstances, do you think you can help? If you can, she'll be coming to you within the next couple of hours or so and, given the circs, will have absolutely nothing with her. The fire brigade won't allow anyone back in there until their own investigations have been completed. And, by the sound of it, there might not be much that's salvageable in any case. Sounds like it was a pretty major conflagration. They are both very lucky to be alive.'

'Yes, of course,' I said, glancing across the landing at the bedroom recently vacated by young Ethan. I'd stripped the bed, and Ethan had actually claimed quite a lot of the decorative items I'd placed in there, but it wouldn't take me long to dress the room suitably for a six-year-old girl. 'What's her name?' I added. 'Sorry, you probably already told me and I missed it – I'm only just properly awake.'

'Me too,' he said. 'Been a long old shift and I'm only halfway through it. And I didn't yet. It's Amelie. Amelie Knight, and … hang on one sec while I just check my screen … ah yes, it will be a social worker bringing her to you, name of Andy Clarke. Will you manage for something for her to wear tonight and possibly tomorrow? Only he's said he doesn't mind looking for a 24-hour supermarket to grab a couple of things for her if you don't have what she needs.'

I smiled. Over the years, between my grandchildren outgrowing good clothes, and my obsession with snapping up bargains (or 'compulsive shopping syndrome',

5

as Mike termed it), I had more outfits than a movie costume department; ones for children of every age and superhero persuasion. All packed neatly away in my landing cupboards and loft. And my heart also went out to the doubtless exhausted on-call social worker, who would, I thought, struggle to find anywhere open, and already had enough on his plate. So I assured Ant that I'd manage, and that I also had a huge collection of toys and arts and craft things.

*Now what to do?* I thought once I'd hung up. Did I wake Mike straight away and tell him what was going on, or did I let him sleep on and instead spend a lovely hour or so cleaning and sorting out a new bedroom first? Cleaning won. Cleaning always wins with me.

Cleaning and, of course, coffee. I'd recently treated myself to a large copper-insulated coffee jug. It was quite expensive, but it held around five mugs of my favourite beverage, and in my opinion was worth every penny. 'It will look so posh on the table when I have meetings,' I'd said as I'd pleaded my case with Mike, 'and even if I don't have many meetings for a bit, think how much more housework I could get done without having to stop every 20 minutes to go back to the kitchen and make a new coffee?' (He'd just nodded and continued watching the football. He knew it made sense, or at least he knew when I set my heart on something, I wasn't going to give up without a fight.)

So I padded downstairs in the dark and made a jug to keep me going and, by the time I stood back to admire my handiwork on the bedroom, realised I'd gone through four mugs of the stuff. Which was fine; it would be a long time before I got back to bed, after all.

Not knowing anything about our new house guest, I'd taken a chance on unicorns. Pink and purple ones, which gambolled gaily across the duvet cover. I'd also added an assortment of pink cushions, and a fluffy pink throw, which I'd folded neatly across the bottom of the bed. I'd also swapped a couple of pictures of cars for ones of animals and placed a selection of soft toys along the window ledge, with a white unicorn – lately the property of my now seven-year-old oldest grand-daughter, Marley Mae – placed on the pillow. It looked warm and welcoming, and, of course, I always did this, but I couldn't help but wonder about the little girl it was done for and how she'd be coping. What kind of state must the poor child be in?

A check of the time revealed it was now a quarter to four. Silly to wake Mike up till I had to, I decided. It was odds-on she'd be here soon and, given the time, chances were she'd be shattered, so, hopefully, I'd be able to get her straight into bed without waking him at all, which would mean an extra pair of hands if I needed a power nap in the morning.

After pulling out a couple of storage boxes of assorted girls' clothing, which we could sort through tomorrow (assuming nothing was retrievable), I then went back downstairs and into our little front room – the 'snug' –

to look out for them, rather than wait for the sound of the doorbell. We'd not long moved, and Mike had fitted one of those front doorbells that came with a camera and an app, so that, if you were out, you could see who'd come calling. (Or had lied about having tried to deliver your parcel, which was what most people seemed to want them for.) It was a fun novelty, but the bell itself was noisy. No point tiptoeing around all this time only to have him woken up anyway. Happily, a car pulled up only a couple of minutes later, so I tightened the cord on my dressing gown, placed a mask on my face and went to open the front door.

You never know what to expect at such times, but, given what I knew about the child's situation, I had at least some idea; that she'd be exhausted-looking, lost and afraid. However, the sight that greeted me was nothing like that. In fact, I was so surprised by what I saw the first time I met Amelie that I even started back-tracking through the recent contents of my brain. Had I got the story straight or had I dreamt it?

For she was like a pink pyjama-clad whirlwind. The very moment she was released from her seatbelt, she jumped out of the social worker's car, reached back in to grab something, then was up the path like a pocket rocket, whereupon she flung her arms around my hips, a massive smile on her face.

'Oh, wow,' I said, smiling down and stroking soft, russet-blonde shoulder-length curls. 'What a lovely, lovely welcome!'

I glanced at Andy, eyebrows raised, and he seemed to understand. He raised his own in response, with a bemused shake of his head, seemingly at a loss to explain this odd reaction, too.

The girl finally released me, then stepped back and beamed, her smile into my eyes almost unnervingly direct. 'Can I see my room, please?' she asked. Then, brandishing what turned out to be a colouring book with an integral place for coloured pencils, 'I'm doing you a picture. It's really pretty. Andy said so.'

She turned her gaze towards him now. 'It is indeed,' he reassured her. 'And I'm sure you'll see your room soon enough. Now, how about we first go inside,' he added, as I stood back to allow them both to enter. 'And then I'll help you find the page so we can show Casey what you've done for her.' He held out a hand, which she took, and without a moment's hesitation either, which made me wonder if they'd already met. Perhaps EDT hadn't been aware when they'd called me, but, if it was true about the mum having mental health problems, perhaps the family were already known to social services. Either way, I would find out soon enough, I supposed.

I led them both into the open-plan living space at the back, where the girl, once again with a curious lack of inhibition, made a beeline for the large corner sofa. The way she'd spoken, in fact her manner generally, was slightly odd for a six-year-old, and, as Andy bent down to settle her (she'd now announced that she'd like to finish colouring her picture), I wondered if she had some learning difficulties. If she did it might explain some of this strange behaviour in reaction to what she had surely suffered, but still it all seemed very odd. She'd just been pulled from a raging fire, hadn't she?

And it seemed Andy had only met her for the first time two hours ago. 'I'm baffled,' he admitted, having joined me in the kitchen area. 'She's been like this from the moment I picked her up.' He explained that when he'd got there, they hadn't known where he'd be taking her, so they'd waited in an office, with an activity box they'd provided in case the child needed distracting at all. 'She was straight into it,' he said, 'drew a heart and a rainbow, wrote "I love you" across it and said it was for me. And she's never stopped chattering away, laughing, smiling – even dancing! I tell you, I've never seen anything quite like it. And when you think about the circumstances … it's all pretty weird, if you ask me.'

From what I could see behind his own mask, Andy, I judged, was in his late twenties or early thirties, and though I knew nothing about him, because our paths had never crossed, he definitely didn't strike me as inexperienced or naive. Just, as I was, a little nonplussed by the child's odd behaviour. He also confirmed he knew nothing more about Amelie than I did.

I admitted that I hadn't seen anything quite like it either. 'But we'll find out soon enough, I guess,' I said. 'Or not,' I corrected myself, because if she wasn't in the system, had no immediate family and Mum was currently hospitalised, then all I had to go on was what I had in front of me, and unfortunately nothing as yet made any sense.

We got the form signed (just a standard form with Amelie's full name and date of birth, her mother's name, and their address – there was obviously no care plan as yet), by which time Andy was yawning and keen to head off, leaving Amelie in my care.

She hugged Andy as if he was a cherished older brother and, once he'd gone, after wolfing down three biscuits and a carton of juice, was more than happy to go and see her new room, greeting the scene before her with a wide-eyed, 'Oh, *wow*!'

Then curiously, she flung her arms out and did a melodramatic yawn. It was almost as if she'd watched a 'how to demonstrate a yawn' video on YouTube. It took no time at all then to get her into a pair of my stock of pyjamas; she was as trusting of my help as one of my own grandkids, and not at all fazed to be ushered into an unfamiliar bed. 'I'm so *tired*,' she exclaimed, slipping happily underneath the unicorn-covered duvet at once. 'I love my room,' she added. 'Thank you *very* much!' then reached for a hug, and pursed her tiny rosebud lips for a kiss too. This was very, very unusual, but I did as any woman in my shoes would do, and gave the child a quick peck on the cheek, a big smile and a warm hug.

'You get some sleep, sweetie,' I said as I left the room and gently closed the door.

I paused outside our room and wondered if now was the time to wake Mike and tell him about our most unusual house guest, but I stopped myself. It was, after all, only just gone 5.00 a.m. still.

More coffee, then. My news could wait for another couple of hours. So I slipped my mask off and padded back downstairs, reflecting that, whatever transpired in the morning, my 'new normal' had just become anything but.

# Chapter 2

Decades of getting up at the same obscenely early time every morning meant that Mike found it impossible to sleep in. I wasn't quite so regimented in my own habits, so he was naturally surprised to wake up and not find me fast asleep beside him, particularly given that for the past fortnight, since that chilling announcement 'You must stay at home', we had been living in a weird parallel universe which meant neither of us had anything to get up *for*.

He was even more surprised to see me sitting at the breakfast bar (with so much caffeine on board there was no possibility of going back to bed and actually sleeping) and scrolling through my social media at 6.30 in the morning.

He was, however, not terribly surprised to hear that, while he'd been snoring away, totally oblivious, we'd taken in a new child via EDT.

'Well, it was only ever going to be a matter of time, wasn't it?' was his pronouncement while I made him a coffee. 'There must be a massive shortage of people willing to do respite care right now. And I reckon that's only going to get worse as this goes on, since everyone is beginning to realise older people are more at risk. Lots of us are our kind of age, *and* older, aren't they and even the ones that aren't – some will have caring commitments for older family members, and people like that just won't want to risk bringing strangers into their homes.' He took his coffee. 'And there's the rub, isn't it? Because with this whole lockdown business and all the stress that's going with it, there's probably a similarly large increase in kids needing it, too. Anyway, what's the story with this one?'

I gave him the lowdown, little of it though there was as yet, while I set about making us both some breakfast. Yes, it was still early, but we'd made a pact not to fall into slothful habits. With nothing much to do, and absolutely nowhere to go, it would be all too easy to while the days away sitting around and watching telly, so we'd decided to stick to some kind of routine. Getting up, getting dressed, getting out into the garden. And with the weather so nice, I'd even tabled the idea that, rather than veg out, we might even start growing our own veg. We had more than enough space in the garden, after all.

Mike laid us places at the breakfast bar (another novelty for us) while I fetched some eggs out of the cupboard and filled a saucepan with water.

'Odd,' he agreed, once I'd filled him in on Amelie's strange response to the traumas she'd been through.

'But maybe the reality won't kick in till she wakes up. Maybe last night her brain went into some kind of protective override or something. I mean, that sort of thing can happen, can't it?'

I considered that. Mike was right, of course. The human brain was amazing and had lots of protective tricks up its sleeve, but what I'd witnessed from Amelie just didn't seem like that. Not in the usual way, at least. Something was telling me that her presentation, what I'd seen of her, wasn't like that. It felt more like a normal rather than reactive behaviour. But still, after a trauma like a house fire, which must have been absolutely terrifying, it was hard to imagine that she wouldn't have been severely affected by it, so perhaps he was right. We might see a complete change in her when she woke up.

'I just don't know,' I admitted as I dropped slices of bread into the toaster. 'It's just a guessing game right now.'

He chuckled. 'Isn't it always?'

I nodded. 'But perhaps by the time I call Christine, she'll have gathered some more intel. Maybe the mum will have been able to shed a little more light, or she'll have sleuthed out a bit more background for us. I can't believe there isn't some family out there somewhere.'

I wasn't holding my breath on the intel front, however, not with everything else that was going on, but I knew it wouldn't be for lack of trying. We'd worked alongside Christine Bolton, our supervising social worker, for quite a few years now, and we knew each other pretty well, so I knew that she'd be concerned that we'd agreed to a placement in the early hours, without having the chance to really think about it, or indeed consider if Amelie was a suitable fit for our family. Christine was incredibly conscientious, and had a genuine desire to keep her fostering 'crew' happy. Knowing we'd gone ahead, she would, I was sure, be on the case already, to find out as much as possible and to give us any help she could.

I wasn't disappointed. By the time I called her, at just after nine, she was fully up to speed. And though she hadn't yet had time to find out any more for us about the family she assured me that by the time she made her visit to us at lunchtime, she'd have dug up as much as she could. 'And when I get to yours later, we'll put a proper plan in place,' she said, 'because there is nothing at this point to suggest that Amelie is going to be scooped up by a loving relative this morning. So, her stay with you might not be a short one. And there's plenty to suggest we might be talking a month at the very least, as Mum, given the mental health aspect, might well have been sectioned. By the way, our kid, should I bring my own mug and teabags?'

I laughed. Christine had been born and bred in Liverpool, and I could listen to her soft, sing-song accent all day long. I assured her I still had a stock of teabags – *and* loo roll – and though we'd obviously have to observe the new 'social distancing' rules, that I thought I was still allowed to dig out my own teabags and make her a cup of that foul brew she loved.

'Pots and kettles,' she said before hanging up.

Mike was now washed and dressed, and with Amelie still catching up on all those hours of missed sleep he was decked out in his 'projects in the garden' attire, clothes that were basically fit for the rag bag, and rootling in a kitchen drawer for his shed keys. While I was set on taking the opportunity to grow swathes of tomatoes and runner-bean plants, he planned to use the lockdown to make a start on a brand new project to cheer me up, namely building a base and an enclosure for a hot tub.

And I needed cheering up, too. I had, the previous autumn, planned and booked a large villa in Spain for a big family holiday. And I mean big. We had saved for a year, just so we could treat everyone, and everyone was booked to come – all my kids and their partners, all my grandchildren, and my mum and dad too, since instinct told me this could be their last chance. Up until the last couple of weeks, I'd clung on to hope that the whole pandemic nonsense would be over in time for us to still go on it. However, once it looked as if it wasn't, I'd made an executive decision – to buy both ourselves, and the kids, an inflatable hot tub instead. At least, I thought, it would ensure we all had some fun, and with a soak in the hot weather, and a cocktail or two, we could pretend we were somewhere exotic.

It did the trick; it was nothing grand, but I was ridiculously excited. Mike had promised me fairy lights, a changing area and a hand-built table made out of decking boards that would curve around the outside of it, for the use of drinks and snacks, while we enjoyed, as he put it, our 'peaceful lockdown retreat'. I was thrilled, and he was right. Though it was still a tad early to be dancing round the garden in swimwear, this unseasonably hot weather was the perfect excuse to hop into a hot tub, and to get out into the garden and soak up the sun. (Though I'd give it a few more days before telling him that a new decking area for doing just that was going to be the next on my agenda.)

Amelie was still snoring softly in her bed when Christine arrived just after noon, by which time, as if in defiance of the hated virus, the sun was already shining down with Spanish levels of intensity. It was good, I thought, that the poor little thing was getting lots of sleep after the awful events of the night before.

'It's still strange though,' I told Christine, once we were both settled in the garden to chat, albeit the requisite two metres apart across the garden table. (That was one good thing, I thought, about taking on a placement. As designated key workers we were at least allowed to interact.) 'The little mite didn't seem at all fazed about any of it. Never asked who I was, where she was, or even anything about her mummy. And after everything that happened. Don't you think that's odd?'

Christine nodded. 'On the face of it, yes. But after

what I've learned this morning, maybe not as odd as you might think.'

'Ah,' I said. 'So you've managed to find out some background about the family?'

'I have indeed.'

'So, are they known to you, then?'

'Well, as it turns out, apparently yes – though I've literally just found that out. And our involvement with the family is only very recent. In fact, the family have only been in our area for a short while. Anyway, it seems the head teacher at Amelie's school shared her concerns about Mum with us a couple of weeks back, and someone had already had a conversation with her GP, and medically, as in mental health wise, there is indeed a history.'

And a sad one, it seemed.

Amelie's mother, Kelly, had bipolar disorder, and had apparently been suffering with it for some time. Although she was being treated with powerful medication, the nature of the disease meant that she often refused to take her meds, convinced that doctors were trying to either subdue or to poison her.

'Her main thing,' Christine explained, 'which has been going on now for a while apparently, is that she believes the FBI are having her followed, and that they have been bugging her house. Amelie's school got in touch because they had begun to be concerned about her welfare. Mum would often keep her at home, and when she did take her in, she would act very bizarrely, hiding Amelie beneath her coat till everyone else had gone into school, and returning her reading diary with odd symbols drawn on it, rather than her signature.'

I glanced upward towards the bedroom windows, thinking about the poor little thing tucked up in her new temporary bedroom, and how frightening and bewildering it must have been for her, seeing her mother's mind unravelling the way it clearly had. 'And what about the fire? Any news on how it started?'

'It's a little early to get it confirmed by the fire service, but I understand Mum was very clear anyway. She told them that she'd set fire to the house deliberately.' Christine shook her head. 'I was thinking on my way over that she could have easily killed both of them, so this is a very lucky outcome. And you know, if it wasn't for the lockdown, and so much work having been postponed, chances are that there would have been some sort of intervention already – Amelie was so clearly at risk, wasn't she? But on the other hand, perhaps the lockdown was also a blessing. Apparently the neighbour told one of the paramedics that he was supposed to be in Tenerife this week. He was joking that he was after a bit of heat to warm his bones, but not as a result of next door burning down! Funny how life works out sometimes, eh?'

'It sure is,' I agreed. 'Someone must be looking out for that little one upstairs, mustn't they? And did Mum say *why* she needed to try and burn the house down?'

Christine nodded. 'Yes. She was absolutely convinced that an agent was in her home yesterday. For some reason, she'd covered all the windows with aluminium foil and then basically set about trashing the house, looking for clues about what they were up to, apparently. Amelie had taken herself off to bed, presumably to get out of the way, but woke up when she heard her mother screaming for agents to show themselves. It took the poor kid quite a while to find her mum; she'd started the fire in the living room, but Amelie apparently found her hiding in the downstairs loo and led her outside to safety. Poor woman was only wearing her knickers, apart from a layer of tin foil she'd wrapped around her head.'

'So was Amelie interviewed then? Has all of this come from her?' I asked.

'Mainly the neighbours, as well as the mother's ramblings, which didn't make a lot of sense, but, yes, Amelie apparently filled in some of the blanks when she was talking with the paramedics on scene.'

I could barely believe what I was hearing. It sounded like something from a science-fiction movie. 'But surely the girl's mother knew her daughter was in there and at risk of being killed?'

'According to the hospital,' Christine said, 'she wouldn't have been in any state to even think about her daughter at such a manic stage. She was way beyond any coherent thoughts; she even started to accuse the doctors and nurses of being part of the conspiracy. She told them she started the fire to try to destroy any bugging devices that she knew for a fact had been hidden around her home. After she was checked out and treated for smoke inhalation, she was immediately sectioned under the Mental Health Act and was transferred for a mandatory 28-day stay at a facility in Manchester.'

Manchester was many, many miles from where we lived, and I wondered about the logistics of taking Amelie to visit her mother there. But then it kicked in. Given the Covid restrictions, would she even be allowed to visit her? I imagined not. There were already lots of reports of people not even being able to visit dying relatives, and having to have those precious last conversations via iPads the medical staff held up for them. I also picked up on the 28-day thing.

'So, you were right then,' I said. 'About her being sectioned. And the mandatory 28-day thing, is that how long this placement will be then? I mean, presumably, once Mum is back on her meds, Amelie will be returned to her, presumably with lots of support put in place. Or would there still be too much risk for that to happen?'

'Well, your guess is as good as mine at this stage, obviously. Mum might be in hospital for months. Of course, it could be that after the 28 days they have her back on track and with ongoing support ...' Christine spread her hands. 'But in reality, who knows? Given what's just happened, and the fact that she'd already come into the system before the pandemic, my hunch is that they would have to be very, very sure that she had sufficient capacity – and, well, even if they deemed her capable of living independently, to be responsible for a *child* ... That's a whole other scenario, isn't it? So, bottom line, if you do decide you're happy to take Amelie on, it would need to be on the grounds that it's completely open-ended. An indefinite placement. Which, I know, under the circumstances isn't something to take on lightly.'

Christine was certainly right about that. But, at the same time, were it not for the pandemic, it didn't feel particularly daunting. We were always in it for the long haul, unless there was good reason for that not to be the case. Apart from a few specific periods when family matters took precedence and we elected to do some periods providing only respite, that was what we did – took kids in until they could either go back to their own families or were found long-term foster homes to see them through to adulthood, or adoptive parents. We'd begun as specialist 'crisis' foster carers, given extra training to deal with particularly challenging children, and though that whole programme had been retired a few years previously (almost certainly due to budget cuts), we were more often than not on the 'to call' list when those particularly challenging children came along.

Amelie definitely didn't sound as though she fitted that category so there was no reason not to be in this for however long it took. I said so.

'Ah, and that reminds me,' Christine said, 'I wanted to talk to you about helping out with a bit of respite care as well. Was already going to this week, actually, as we were wondering if you could commit to doing some short periods of cover for other foster carers as well. I know it's a big ask, especially in these uncertain times, when we can't get out and about to properly support everyone, but that's the problem. A lot of carers have teenagers living with them right now – a few of them pretty problematic – and some are going a bit stir-crazy. As well as that, as you can imagine, I'm sure, the carers are struggling to keep teens indoors, especially when they're in an area where they've made friends. It's proving really stressful, what with all the inevitable arguments that ensue, and there's nowhere to go to get away from it. So, we've got our heads together and have put together a scheme whereby we swap children around if we can during this time – one, so that they're out of area and don't have the pull of mates to make them leave the house, and, two, just to give carers a bit of a break if they need it. The kids as well of course, giving credence to the old adage "a change is as good as a rest". Hopefully. Fingers crossed and all that.'

I nodded as she spoke. It did make sense, and, really, we carers were an 'at risk' group anyway, since we were bringing in children from other families. But I supposed if as much protection as possible were put in place, then we didn't really have much choice. Or should we, for that matter. It was our job to step up, after all, and the pandemic didn't stop the break-up of families, did it? In

Little Girl Lost

fact, as Mike had already commented earlier, it was almost certainly contributing to it, and particularly in this case. I could only imagine what sort of horrors Amelie's mum must have been thinking about if she already had conspiracy theories running around her head.

'Of course,' I said. 'In for a penny and all that. And having Mike home makes a massive difference.'

Mike's voice chipped in. 'Is that my name I hear being taken in vain?' he said, as he emerged from the house, having just been inside to get his drill back off its charger. 'I just went up to check – little one's still blotto, by the way.'

'You did indeed,' Christine told him. 'Casey's just been signing your life away. Well, for the immediate future anyway.'

I explained about the open-ended nature of taking on Amelie, and that we'd be happy – well, that *I* was – about adding the odd challenging teen into the mix here and there. 'If *you're* happy, that is,' I added.

He laughed. 'So pretty much business as usual then,' he said. 'Except I don't get to escape to the sanity of work every day.' He shrugged. Then did a whirr of the newly charged drill. 'So, in the words of Chief Brody – you know, him off *Jaws* – it looks like we're gonna need a bigger hot tub. Or at least,' he added, 'a bigger table. Though with a houseful of kids again, I think we can safely say goodbye to the "peaceful lockdown retreat" bit.'

'Woah! I never said anything about a houseful!' I said in horror. I looked at Christine, who was grinning like the cat that had got the cream. 'Just one or two at a time, please.'

'Deal,' she said. 'And I really cannot thank you both enough. Now I just have to get a few more foster carers to see the light, and this scheme will be good to go.'

And I was happy to help out. I knew Mike was as well. This wasn't just a complicated and demanding time for Christine, after all. I'd cared for enough challenging teens to know that, for some of us, this lockdown would prove to be *extremely* difficult to cope with. A world away from caring for just one little six-year-old.

'Who wants a peaceful lockdown retreat anyway?' I quipped.

Mike wielded the drill again. 'Hmm,' he quipped back as he strode back across the garden. 'I say be careful what you wish for ...'

# Chapter 3

It was a good hour after Christine left that Amelie finally stirred. I'd popped up to check on her a couple of times in the interim but, though she was clearly sweaty in her fleecy pyjamas – the weather was once again ridiculously warm – she was obviously catching up on a lot of missed sleep, and looked very peaceful and angelic as she slumbered the morning away.

But if I'd thought Amelie would be traumatised by waking up and finding herself in an unfamiliar bedroom, and suddenly among strangers, I thought wrong. Instinct had told me that her odd, ebullient behaviour when she'd arrived with us was probably down to shock, or even hysteria, and that she'd be either shut down or distraught once her new reality sank in. To my surprise, though, she was nothing of the sort.

I was halfway up the stairs when she appeared on the landing, hopping from foot to foot and clearly in need of a wee.

'Oh, you're awake, sweetie!' I said, as I hurried up the last few steps and pointed her in the direction of the bathroom. 'In there,' I added, ushering her ahead of me. 'I'll be just outside.'

'I'm busting!' she announced, then, rather perplexingly, 'and you haven't got no bowl or nothing.' She then proceeded to yank her pyjamas bottoms down and hop up onto the toilet.

I pulled the door to, in order to give her some privacy, but she clearly didn't want any. 'Don't shut the door!' she ordered, panic evident in her tone. 'I don't like the door being shut!'

'That's fine,' I began. 'I'll just –'

'And don't go away!'

'I won't go away,' I reassured her. 'I'm right here, I promise. Standing just outside the door.'

I heard the flush go moments later and the sound of a tap running. A good sign, I mused. So, she obviously wasn't feral. She'd had her hand hygiene drilled in at least.

The door opened moments later, though she was opening it with her foot, her hands occupied in being vigorously shaken. I reached around her and grabbed a hand towel from the rack, but she recoiled from it. 'I mustn't touch that,' she said, shaking her head firmly. Then considered. 'Not 'less it's been microwaved. Has it been microwaved?'

'No,' I said, trying and failing to grasp what she was on about. 'We don't put towels in the microwave. But it *has* been in the tumble dryer.'

This didn't seem to impress her. 'But you have to microwave it to kill all the poison.'

Ah, I thought. It seemed I was going to have quite a lot to learn. 'It's fine,' I said. 'We have a special tumble dryer, and it does that as well. It's quite safe.' I proffered it again.

'Okay,' she said, as if accepting that I was telling her the truth. She took it. Then, as she diligently dried her hands, added, 'they have those air dryer things at school. I'm not s'posed to touch them as well because they actually *blow out* poison. But Miss Parsons says they're special ones so they're okay to use as well. So, I do,' she finished, handing the towel back to me. 'Sometimes I do, anyway. Don't tell Mummy though. She'll go totally *crayyyyzee*.'

Unsure how to respond to that, but adding it to the mental picture I was painting, I folded the towel and slipped it back over the towel rack. But even as I was formulating a suitably non-committal response, she grabbed my sleeve and said, 'Miss, do you have any food in? Like stuff for breakfast?'

Safer ground. And, since she'd only just got up, a reasonable enough question, even if by now it was mid-afternoon. 'It's Casey,' I told her, smiling. 'And yes, indeed we do. All sorts of things. Come on, let's head downstairs and see what we can find. What sort of food do you most like to eat?'

By the time we were downstairs I had quite the list. She liked beans. But not spaghetti. She liked toast. She liked bacon. She liked chocolate-coloured cereal and she liked dippy eggs. She liked water but not from taps. Only from 'bottles with their tops on', the reasons for which I was beginning to understand now, but decided not to enquire about just yet.

'How about orange juice from little cartons with straws that come attached to them?' I asked her, while she cast her assessing gaze around as we walked down the hallway, rather like an estate agent valuing a house. 'You know,' I added, 'like you had when you got here?'

'They are fine,' she said nodding, by which time we had arrived in the kitchen diner, and, spotting Mike out in the garden, she gasped and clutched at my sleeve. 'Who's that man?'

'That's Mike,' I said. 'He's my husband.'

'Does he live here?'

'Yes, he does. And he's been very much looking forward to meeting you. Tell you what, let's go and say hello to him, shall we?'

I took her across to the large bifold doors. They were as high as the ceiling and spanned almost the whole back of the house. We'd been in this one less than a year and I still wasn't used to them. They just felt so big and so ridiculously grand.

I called to Mike, who, having noticed us, put down the length of wood he was brandishing.

'Well, hello, Amelie,' he said, waving and smiling as he crossed the garden to join us. 'I'm Mike. Very pleased to meet you.'

Amelie still held onto my sleeve, clearly anxious in his presence. And fair enough, I thought. With the sun behind him, and with his height and bulk, Mike must have cut quite an imposing figure for a nervous little girl. Which he seemed to sense because, once he reached us, he immediately squatted down.

She shrank back a little, drawing closer against me, and as well as the heat of her body pressed against me, I could detect a faint whiff of smoke coming off her hair. But then her curiosity won out. 'What you doing?' she asked him. 'Are you making something?'

'I am indeed,' he said. 'I'm making a base for a hot tub.' He swivelled slightly to point. 'To put over there.'

'What's a hot tub?'

'Well, I suppose it's like a kind of paddling pool, but for grown-ups.'

Amelie considered this. 'Can't children go in it?'

'Well, maybe. We'll see. But, you know, we also have a paddling pool *just* for little ones like you.'

'I'm not little,' she said, immediately pulling herself up to her full height. 'I'm six, an' I'm gonna be seven next year.'

Mike grinned. 'So you are. Well, our paddling pool is fine for six-year-olds too. Tell you what,' he said, glancing up at me. 'There's a thought. Since it's such a lovely day, why don't I see about getting it out and filling it up for you? Would you like that?'

Amelie nodded at this but then reconsidered. 'But not till I've had breakfast.' She sighed a weary sigh and looked up at me. 'I'm *so* hungry. Can I *please* get some food, miss?'

Mike grinned and stood up. 'You and me both, kiddo. Can I *please* get some food as well, miss?'

So, 15 minutes later, our alfresco mid-afternoon breakfast was served. Which was actually fine – with no work schedule, or school schedule, or any difference between weekdays and weekends, why the devil not have a cooked breakfast at three in the afternoon? So, we had eggs, bacon and beans, and a pile of toast to go with it, and we got our first proper taste of our singular little house-guest, who clearly had some issues around food.

With her own plate of food polished off in a matter of minutes, Amelie sat back in her chair with another of those world-weary sighs, and stared intently at mine and Mike's.

'Are you still hungry, sweetie?' I asked her.

She nodded. 'I'm *starving*.'

'Here,' I said, transferring some bacon and a slice of toast from my plate to hers. 'And I can always make you some more toast. It's probably been a long time since you had a proper meal, after all.'

Amelie duly wolfed both toast and bacon down, and then looked over at Mike. 'Have you got any food spare?' she asked him.

He looked down at his almost-empty plate. 'Only a few beans, but –'

She lifted both her hands and made grasping motions with her fingers. 'Gimme, gimme!' she said excitedly.

'Me want! Me want! Me hungy hungy baby! Wahh, wahh, wahhhhh!'

Mike and I exchanged a glance. Where had this odd baby talk suddenly come from?

He pushed his plate across the table, and she stretched across to grab it. 'Beany beany, lemoneeny,' she babbled, before polishing off the handful of baked beans as well, using her fingers to scoop them faster onto her fork.

'Well,' I said, smiling at her. 'You really *were* hungry, weren't you? How about I fetch you some fruit and a yoghurt? For afters,' I added, as Mike started clearing plates.

But Amelie clung on to Mike's plate and, having dumped her knife and fork beside it, picked it up and proceeded to lick it completely clean, before setting it down with a deep, drawn-out 'Ahhhhh ...' a small smear of bean juice glistening at the end of her pixie-like little nose.

We exchanged another glance, both of us knowing the other's cogs were whirring. We had only the scantest of background details to go on, but just a couple of hours with Amelie had already flagged a fair few oddities. There was clearly going to be a lot, as they say, to 'unpack'.

Over the years, we'd looked after a number of children who had had issues with and difficulties around food. More than one of our foster kids had had issues with hoarding – sneaking food from the kitchen and secreting things away, or compulsively shoplifting sweets and chocolate when in shops. These often stemmed from early childhoods that had involved great neglect and genuine panic about when they might next eat. With our first foster child, Justin, it was perhaps his biggest challenge. So much so that we had to maintain a chart in the kitchen, detailing what meals we'd be having and when we'd be having them, and, in the early months, if we didn't adhere to it, and to the very minute, it could trigger a violent, and deeply distressing, meltdown.

With other children it had been issues around certain types of food. Phobias, almost, around specific feared items; we'd had one child, a little boy who had undiagnosed autism, who would only eat food that was white. In some cases, it was a more straightforward problem with socialising. Most people take basic etiquette for granted, but if children came from situations where no socialising had ever happened, how could they possibly understand things like table manners?

Amelie seemed at first to be a mix of all three, and it was impossible to say how much was nature and how much nurture. Some of it, at least, seemed quite obvious. Her mum's mental health issues had almost certainly played a part in her odd pronouncements and reasoning; if her mum told her the water that came out of the kitchen tap might be poisoned then why, as a small trusting child, would she not believe her? Even the more slightly odd business of microwaving towels to kill poison (a first for me, definitely) would probably, to Amelie's young mind, feel perfectly reasonable, if that was what she'd been told was the reason and was all she knew. And there was obviously a whole world of things we *didn't* know yet. About how they had lived, how their day-to-day lives were conducted, what fears about the wider world her mum, with her illness, had passed down to her little girl to be accepted as facts.

But I had a strong hunch that Amelie was more complex than that. Yes, we could gently teach her table manners, and allay her various conspiracy theory-related fears, but it was her general demeanour, the random segueing into baby babble and her apparent lack of interest in where her mother was that, as the day went on, concerned me the most. Apart from her one comment that her mother would go 'crayyyzeee' if she found out she'd used the hand dryers at school, Amelie hadn't even mentioned her. Not once. On the face of it, she'd been transplanted from her burning home in the small hours, and deposited with total strangers, and had just accepted it. No tears. No questions. No apparent distress. Why? With everything she knew ripped so suddenly and completely from her life, surely at some point, it would hit home?

In the meantime, we could only watch and wait, and try to figure her out. Though, by the time I went to bed that night, it was with the feeling that there was precious little sense to be made of her. I had pretty much decided I'd allow her to dictate the pace. If she asked questions,

I would answer them, and if she became distressed, I would try to comfort her, but I wouldn't probe or prod – I would let her take the lead.

But none came. If anything, it was as if Amelie saw her new situation as a kind of planned holiday. Mike duly got out the paddling pool and I found her a swimming costume from my vast array of 'just in case' clothing, and she enjoyed splashing about till it grew dark. She then came indoors and spent a good hour engrossed in drawing and colouring, creating brightly coloured pictures of hearts and flowers and rainbows – the very antithesis of the kind of dark, upsetting pictures stereotypically produced by psychologically troubled kids.

Her appetite was simply incredible. She demanded food often (and often with her melodramatic sighs, and/ or the baby babble) and when we had tea – a rather late one – she actually tried to snatch food off our plates. Which was strange in itself. She wasn't skinny, but she wasn't particularly overweight either, which hinted to this not being her normal appetite or intake, because if she had carried on the way she had for any length of time, she'd be clinically obese in very short order. So, was this compulsive eating, in fact, her 'cry for help'?

It was the following morning, though, when I got the clearest sense yet of what made Amelie tick.

We'd woken late – it was close to eight before I got out of bed and the first thing I heard was the faint sound of humming. Not a song, quite, just a melodious warbling, as her voice danced lightly up and down the scales.

I went into her bedroom to find her dusting the windowsill, and with a duster she must have gone down and fetched from the kitchen, along with, I then noticed, a dustpan and brush, a window squeegee, a can of polish and my anti-bac spray. It reminded me immediately of the scene from the movie *Annie*, where all the orphans were scrubbing floors and singing about it being a 'hard knock life'.

She hadn't yet noticed me, so I stood in the doorway and watched, as, still humming to herself, she lifted each item from the sill and carefully wiped it, along with the place where it sat, before putting it down again and moving on to the next thing.

She was already dressed, in one of my granddaughter Marley-Mae's old T-shirt and shorts sets, and the bed, I noticed, had already been beautifully made; in fact, made to a standard a high-end hotel would approve of, down to the pyjamas neatly folded on top of the pillow. It was then that I noticed the boxes. The two storage boxes of clothes I'd got out in readiness before she'd got to us and which I'd riffled through to find a couple of bits for her to wear the previous day. We'd discussed, just last night, that one of the jobs we'd do today would be to sort through them and pick out the things she liked the look of.

Both were in the corner, near the door, and were empty.

'Morning, love,' I said. 'You're up bright and early.'

She spun around, her free hand flying to her chest. 'Oh, you scareded me!' she said.

I smiled and crossed the room. 'I heard you humming,' I said. 'It made me think of Cinderella.' Well, I couldn't say orphan Annie, could I? 'And goodness me, it looks like you've been a busy girl!'

'I'm doing my cleaning,' she said. 'Everything nice and everything in its place.'

She'd spoken that last part as if reciting a mantra. One she'd heard many times before. I wondered where.

'So I see,' I said, going to sit down on the pristine bed but immediately thinking better of it. 'And where have all the clothes gone? Have you put them all away?'

Amelie put down her duster and went over to the chest of drawers, pulling out each of them in turn, so she could show me. 'I have,' she said. 'See? All my socks are in here, and my pants, and my jimjams. And my T-shirts are *here*, and the shorts are all *here*. And I didn't know whose stuff is the stuff at the bottom, so I left all that there, and put the things that don't fit me in that drawer as well.' She turned and beamed up at me, her big pale blue eyes wide with the pleasure of accomplishment.

I could only look on in wonder. The socks were all rolled. The pants were in a neat pile. The tops were all folded not in half but in thirds, so they sat as proudly as if on a shop display. There wasn't a single thing out of place.

'Wow,' I said, genuinely impressed. 'That's amazing! It's not often we have visitors as tidy as you are. And what a busy bee you've been, making everything so lovely!'

'I did my books too,' she said, pulling on my dressing-gown sleeve to direct me. 'See? If you put them in a different order it makes them look like a sort of rainbow.'

It did too. She'd rearranged them all so the coloured spines moved correctly through the colour wheel. ''cept that one, 'cos it's white,' she pointed out. 'So I put it on the end.'

'Well,' I said, 'I must say, it all looks *very* pretty.'

And then I found myself suddenly a little lost for words, it hitting me hard that this was *not* this child's bedroom, or her clothes, or her books. That her own room, her own clothes, her own books were all gone. Or at least, to my knowledge, they were, and I couldn't imagine that they'd manage to salvage anything much, as those not burnt would be water damaged, surely? It was heartbreaking to think about. And yet, about that, and so much else, not a word was being said by this singular little girl. Was now the time to broach that? In any small way?

Perhaps I should test the water. 'You must feel sad that you don't have your own things –' I started.

Amelie did something unexpected then. She shrugged. 'Mummy already gived them to the bags men,' she said. 'So it's nice. Everything nice and everything in its place.'

I tried to digest what she'd just so matter-of-factly said. 'Bags men?'

'That take the bags. You put them out in the morning. You have to do that so they can take the taminated stuff away.'

'Oh, I see,' I said. Seeing nothing but the extent of the strangeness, and visions of a mother so consumed by her disease that even her daughter's possessions were being summarily dispatched. Just what kind of life had the poor mite been living?

'You're right,' Christine said, when I caught up with her the following afternoon. 'When you put it all together, it sounds as if her life up to now has been pretty damned strange. Incredible what lurks under the radar, isn't it? Has she opened up any more to you?'

I looked down into the garden. I was calling Christine from our bedroom while Mike entertained Amelie by recruiting her as his apprentice, having her hand him screws as he began constructing the hot-tub base, using the lengths of decking wood he'd cut to size the previous day. After her initial reticence around him, Amelie had decided she now 'loved' him, and he had his own picture of hearts and rainbows to prove it. 'Not in any way that makes sense to me,' I said. 'And it's very concerning, I mean *really* concerning. It's as if none of it even happened to her. No mention of the fire, and she still hasn't asked a single thing about where Mum is, or what's happening. Just all this matter-of-fact stuff – these chinks of light into what seems like a pretty chaotic if not disturbing home life. By the way, I was wondering – was anything salvaged from their home?'

'Not that anyone's told me. Though it's still very early days. I'll chase. Though by the sound of it from your log, would there even be anything *to* save?' she added, echoing my own thoughts. 'In any event, I was thinking this morning that, since they've started putting in all these new lockdown services, it might be worth getting Amelie an appointment with a child psychologist; they have this video call set-up – Zoom or Teams, or whatever. Other carers have been saying it's been really beneficial, especially with kids who've suffered traumas. If you're concerned about her mental health, might be worth giving it a go?'

'That's the weird thing; I mean, some of her behaviours and the things she says are odd, very odd, as is the random regressing to toddler-style behaviour. But at the same time she's just so sunny. I just can't get my head around it, to be honest. Perhaps it's me who needs the psychologist! Seriously though, I know everyone's stretched. I wouldn't want to use up a space that could be used for a child who is in distress, but at the same time, the way she is so assiduously controlling her environment makes me anxious in itself. I think I'd really just like some fresh eyes and ears. Anxious as I am not to lead her or confront her about everything, is *not* doing so likely to cause further harm down the line? I don't want to cause her distress, obviously, but she does need to engage with reality at some point. She may already have major attachment issues, and if they are not addressed, that's surely only going to get worse.'

'Agreed,' Christine said. 'Let's get you an appointment. We should also start to think about school.'

'As in *going* to school? Can she?'

'Oh yes, absolutely. A few are fully closed, obviously, but there's provision in quite a few local primaries. Mostly for key workers' children, but also those where safeguarding at home is likely to be an issue. If we can get her a place, I think it's something we should consider. She's going to be with you for at least a month, after all, and even if we can't get her a place right away, it should definitely be an option. Particularly if her previous attendance has been patchy. Another way to get some structure into her life. Not to mention a bit of normality.'

*Normality?* I thought, as we ended the call. It was a weekday, a workday, and Mike was in the garden with his shirt off. Much like many thousands of others, at least those who hadn't been struck down, or had lost a loved one to a global pandemic no one had seen coming, we were living as if in a bubble, the outside world seen only as if through a film, all the things we took completely for granted all swept away, with no notice. Right now, there was no normal at all.

And in the midst of it, there was this little girl, who had definitely lost her home and, even more tragically, by the looks of it, her mother as well.

I stood up, smoothed the bed covers, and picked up my empty coffee jug. All we could do was our best, I supposed, and help Amelie to try and steer a path out of it all. But not back. Her home had gone, so there *was* no back for her. Only onwards and upwards.

I pushed the bedroom window further open, and called down to them both.

'Right – who's for ice cream?'

'Ice cream!!! Ice cream!!! Ice cream!!!' Amelie trilled back up at me. As if *we* were Mum and Dad. As if nothing bad had happened. As if she didn't have a care in the world.

Which, by any measure, was very, very far from normal.

# Chapter 4

Over the next few days, very little seemed to change. My runner bean seedlings were growing nicely on the kitchen windowsill, and the hot-tub base was taking shape, and though I was desperately missing seeing all my children and grandkids, I was at least buoyed by the fine weather and lots of FaceTimes. I'd by now also introduced Amelie to everyone, albeit virtually, and, as seemed to be her way, she'd spent much time making everyone pictures, which I would scan and send so they could print them at home. It was at least a way of keeping her occupied.

Going into a new week, however, we'd made a few subtle changes. Though the first couple of weeks of lockdown had seen us doing what everyone else had seemed to – i.e. adjusting to the new reality by treating it all as a bit of a holiday – watching TV every teatime and hearing the prime minister's grim announcements had, bit by bit, begun to scare the bejesus out of us, particularly when it came to my elderly mum and dad, who were already not in the best of health. It also looked as if this horrible situation wasn't going to change anytime soon so, both for ourselves and for Amelie, we resolved to reintroduce more discipline and structure. The morning alarm would therefore immediately be reinstated, and the days going forward would be properly planned.

The following Monday morning, therefore, Mike was out in the garden by eight thirty, Amelie was dressed and in the lounge area, playing with my collection of elderly Barbie dolls, and I was in the kitchen area, making porridge for everyone, while Alexa, as per usual, blared out my favourite tunes from my golden oldies playlist. This definitely felt more like it.

I was busy stirring the porridge when I felt a tugging on the back of my top. I turned around to see Amelie. She was jabbing her finger towards the front of the house.

'There's a lady at the door,' she said, raising her voice to be heard over the music. 'She got a sparkly mask on her mouth. She says can you go and talk to her.'

I hadn't heard the doorbell, let alone realised Amelie had gone to answer it. Perhaps I had set the volume just a tad too loud. I told Alexa to stop, and tried to remember if I should be expecting someone. I was pretty sure I wasn't.

Amelie followed me through to the hall, towards the open front door, and on seeing me the masked woman immediately stepped back a few paces. Amelie had been right about the 'sparkly' mask too. This one was black but covered in diamantes. I made an immediate mental note to look on Amazon for something similar.

'Hello, Mrs Watson,' she said cheerfully, 'that's assuming that you *are* Mrs Watson?'

'I am indeed,' I confirmed.

'Ah, great. I do apologise for just turning up out of the blue like this,' she added, 'but I live pretty locally and I thought it made sense to stroll round and drop it off for you. Any excuse to get out and about, to be honest.'

It? I must have looked even more puzzled, because I was. 'I'm sorry,' I said, 'I'm not expecting anything.'

'Oh, then *I'm* sorry.' The woman flashed an identity card that was hanging from a purple lanyard around her neck. 'Lucy Smith. I'm one of the ELAC workers. We were asked to provide laptops or tablets to all of our looked-after children who don't have access to education right now. You were meant to get an email. And you obviously didn't. I'm so sorry.' She then nodded downwards, and it was only now that I became aware that there was a wrapped parcel sitting on my doorstep. 'It's just a tablet for now, but if you do need a laptop just give them a call and we'll do our best. Oh,' she added, with what was an unmistakably pained, slightly exasperated expression (the type you can always recognise, mask or not), 'and I sanitised my hands before handling the package, obviously.'

Bloody Covid! I thought as I bent down to pick it up. I smiled at her. 'Well, no, I'm almost positive I didn't get that email, but this will come in very handy, so thank you.'

She smiled back. 'You're very welcome!'

At which point, usual form would be to ask her if she'd like to come in for a cold drink. It was a very hot day to be traipsing the streets, after all. 'I'd love to invite you in …' I began. 'But I don't think it's allowed, so –'

'Oh, it's absolutely not allowed. But thanks anyway. It's such a treat to get out. Such a blessing to be offi-cially *allowed* to. What strange times we live in, eh? Anyway,' she said, lowering her mask a little so she could smile properly at Amelie, who was standing silently just behind me, keeping hold of my top. 'It's for you, poppet. Something to keep you occupied. That'll be nice, won't it?' she added, and when Amelie just continued to stare up at her, her own expression wary, she raised the mask again and turned back to me. 'Hope it's helpful, anyway. They're pretty simple to set up, I think, but any problems just get back in touch. I'll resend that email as soon as I'm home.'

'Is that like an iPad?' Amelie asked once Lucy had gone. 'My mummy had an iPad.' She sighed then. One of her big melodramatic ones. 'But then we didn't anymore. We had to break it.'

'Oh dear. Why did you have to do that?'

'Because it had bugs in it. Mummy saw them.'

Since this was one of the very few times Amelie had spoken about life with her mother, I was obviously eager to learn more.

'So, you and Mummy were looking for bugs in her iPad together then?' I asked, as we headed back to the kitchen. 'How did you feel about that? Was it scary or funny?'

She grinned. 'It was funny. Mummy said there were secret bugs *everywhere*. That's why we had to break it. We tried with screwdrivers,' she added conversationally, 'but that didn't work, so Mummy threw it up into the sky and broke it that way instead. I never saw the bugs come out though, even though it went bash bang on the path – like pshppppammm! I think they might have flown off already.'

What with Amelie's accompanying actions and impressively descriptive sound effects, the vision of Mum throwing it 'up into the sky' was definitely an arresting one. And it seemed clear that Amelie, very reasonably, equated bugs with creepy crawlies. 'Well, in fact, you wouldn't,' I explained, as I got out some scissors with which to open the carefully wrapped package, 'because the kinds of bugs you get in tablets aren't ones anyone *can* see. They're not like insects. They're little glitches, really, that break computers and iPads and so on. Nothing for you to worry about.'

Her brow furrowed a little. 'What's a glitch?'

'Um …' I began, now heading towards territory I didn't fully understand. Was it something to do with coding? 'Sort of like an electronic fault,' I settled on, not wishing, under the circumstances, to add fuel to the fire by mentioning hackers and malicious intent. 'You know. Like when you switch something on and it doesn't work properly, because something's wrong with the way it's been set up.' And almost added 'or when someone puts a virus on a computer', because I thought it automatically, but, again, held my tongue. That would definitely only muddy murky water further.

Amelie was already shaking her head though. 'No, it wasn't like that. The ones we had were *definitely* real bugs,' she told me. She then cupped a hand around her face and added, in a stage whisper, 'Bugs that were in *hiding*. And not just in the iPad. I told you. They were *everywhere*. In Mummy's phone, in the cooker, in the light switches. In the cupboards. Under the bath.' She spread her hands. 'They were just *everywhere*.'

'Well,' I said, freeing the box that contained the tablet from its bag. 'There are definitely no bugs in *this* one. It's straight from the factory and is completely wrapped up, see? So absolutely no bugs could have got in. And once we've had our breakfast, we'll get it set up for you, shall we?'

I wasn't sure if it was the thought of breakfast or the tablet that excited her so much, but either way she watched excitedly as I got the thing out of its multiple layers of packaging, the irony not lost on me that even if there weren't any bugs *inside* this new tablet, there *were* in fact still real, actual bugs to be aware of, and possibly lurking unseen on every surface. And though I hadn't fully subscribed to the 'wipe down every single item that comes over the threshold' idea, if it *were* true that you could catch Covid that way, the threat was very real. Which made me think. What might Amelie's mother have made of all the coverage of the pandemic, had she not been hospitalised, and she and her daughter were still together at home? Chillingly, it also made me realise something else. Had Mum not had that terrible episode that night, Amelie would probably have dipped completely under the radar. But then, did coverage of the pandemic actually trigger it? I itched to ask Amelie something concrete. Prompt her to open up about what happened and try to establish what her feelings had been. All these days had passed yet she still hadn't asked me how her mum even *was*, let alone when she might be returning. And she was still showing no sign whatsoever of missing her.

'So, you think Mummy will be okay about you having this tablet then?' I finally plumped for, as I put it down ready to set up after we'd had breakfast.

Which was when I got more than a glimmer.

'Yes,' she said, nodding decisively. 'Because you're the people where I'll be safe.'

'Well, yes, you are safe, sweetie,' I said, reassuring her automatically. Though needlessly, it seemed, because she'd said it so matter-of-factly. 'Of course you are,' I added. 'But did Mummy actually tell you that?' Another nod. 'That you'd be safe here?'

'Yes,' she said again. 'She said I'd go and stay with some nice people who'd keep me safe while she went to her happy place.'

'Her happy place?'

Another nod then, for the first time, a clear expression of anxiety. 'Isn't she there?'

'Oh, yes, sweetie, she's there. *Definitely* there. Safe in the hospital.'

At which, Amelie nodded, her anxiety seemingly gone as quickly as it had arrived. She then pointed past me to the cooker. 'Can we have breakfast now?' she asked me. 'I'm *starving*.'

Conversation over, then. So strange. But more than anything, so sad.

I'd like to say that I set up the tablet, but that would be a lie, of course. It was Mike, after breakfast, who did all the honours. I envied him that he knew his way so adeptly around all things computers these days. Having done a few courses for work, he certainly knew more than I did. I, who still struggled to even operate my own phone.

'I'll download a few educational games,' he said. 'Age 4 to 6, I think, and how about YouTube Kids? You know that one, Amelie?'

Amelie, who had sat patiently beside him while he got everything sorted, was by now grinning from ear to ear. 'I love YouTube,' she said. 'I learn all my dancing on that. And I watch Alvin and the Chipmunks. It's my favourite favourite favourite.'

And so it turned out to be. Within minutes, despite the glorious weather, she was happily curled up on the sofa, intermittently laughing out loud at back-to-back episodes of her favourite cartoon. And I was happy to let her. By eleven it was already too hot and bright to have her running around for any length of time outside anyway, though with the 'groundhog day' nature of the days right now, and no sign of things changing, it seemed doubly sad that the poor mite wasn't in school. I could only keep my fingers crossed that Christine would indeed be able to get something sorted out for her, as though I knew from what I'd been told that her attendance had been patchy, one of the key things that might help her onto a path towards a better life now would be the day-to-day normality that a school routine would represent, and the chance to form new friendships and be among peers. ELAC – Education for Looked After Children – were certainly no substitute for the real thing, even if they were kind enough to distribute learning materials.

But what was I thinking? There *was* no normality. As things stood, at least till Christine could find her that place, her days would continue to be spent at home, with just Mike and I for company. Though as I looked across to where she was currently quite content, sitting on the sofa with her screen, I wondered what normality meant for her. Had she even had friends? Had there been neighbours who had kids she might have regularly played with? Or, as I suspected might well be a more likely scenario, did she spend all her time at home with Mum, searching for the invisible bugs that were apparently everywhere and trying to evade all the 'bad mens' she'd mentioned? And what, quite, would that life mean for her psyche?

Still, by the sound of things, at least provision was being set up by schools now, so, hopefully, she'd be sent some work to keep her occupied. She certainly needed something to keep her little mind active. Although, as the next couple of days passed in similar vein, Amelie never once complained of being bored. She was clearly used to occupying herself, and happy to do so. But her joy to be engaged in play by someone else (me or Mike being the only options in this case so we took turns) was immense; in that regard she was like a thirsty traveller in a desert who has just spied some water. And since I wasn't similarly happy to leave her to her own devices for long periods, play we did. We played shops, we made dens, we played with dolls, we played schools; it didn't matter what I suggested, she was invariably thrilled, something that made me feel sad in itself. What a terrible toll her mum's mental illness must have taken on the poor girl.

I said as much to Christine when she phoned me towards the end of that second week. 'It's like every day is Christmas,' I told her. 'Being given the tablet, having access to lots of toys and games, just being played with. It doesn't matter what we do, she laps everything up so wholeheartedly. Which is lovely to see, of course, but at the same time it makes me feel so sorry for her.'

'Well, it is what it is, and I hear what you're saying. Though it's a plus that at least she's not running you ragged.'

'No, not at all, bless her. She's as good as gold. Any word on Mum yet? Is she still happy in her happy place?'

'Nothing to report on that front and, to be honest, I doubt there will be till she's been fully assessed and this mandatory 28 days is up. Though I imagine if Mum's *compos mentis* enough to ask for some contact, we'll hear soon enough. I have good news on the school front, by the way. Do you know your local primary?'

I told her the name. 'And it's literally in the road behind our house. I've not had any dealings with them personally yet, but I do know from the local Facebook group that they've been open – at least some of the time, anyway.'

'That's great. If they're open then we can definitely approach them and see if we can get her on roll for a while. What do you think? I mean it might only be for a couple of days a week, or, potentially, half-days, but I'm sure we could swing it.'

'That would be amazing,' I said. 'So who gets in touch? You or me?'

'It'll be our ELAC worker, possibly Lucy Smith, the one who I think brought the iPad to you? We're on a reduced staff at the moment and Lucy seems to be taking on most of the workload for this area,' Christine said. 'She'll pass on your phone number so they can arrange for you to take Amelie for a visit and get her enrolled. Or I will. No one's quite sure who's doing what right now, to be honest – there are so many staff off … Oh, and in other news, your name's been put forward for a half-hour video call with the child psychologist. That'll be next week some time,' she added, 'and don't worry – if you need more than half an hour, that's fine. They won't end the session if it's important to you. Just make sure you have a list of things you want to bring up, and then it's just a chat really, pretty informal. But Amelie can't be there, so you might have to ask Mike to keep her busy.'

'That won't be an issue,' I said. 'Amelie already loves Mike as much as she loves me. He has a huge red love heart with his name in it, stuck to the fridge, just to prove it.'

'Well, I'm feeling left out now.'

'Oh, your turn will come, I'm sure. But, yes, that's not a problem,' I said. 'And thanks, Chris. Progress all round, eh?'

'Indeed. Onwards and upwards. Or, to put it another way, enjoy the calm before the storm. You're down for potential respite next weekend, don't forget.'

'I had forgotten,' I admitted. 'But a change is as good as a rest, eh?' I said, quoting her.

Christine chuckled. 'Hmm … in *theory*.'

# Chapter 5

Over the next few days and nights, the rhythm of our lives didn't really change. We had become used to Amelie's funny little ways now, and she, it seemed, had become used to us.

I was also getting more of a handle on what seemed to inspire bouts of the toddler-talk. And on that front I had made some progress. If she went into 'babble-mode', as I had come to think of it, when it was just the two or three of us, a gentle reminder – 'Amelie, you are six, darling, not two, please act like a big girl' – would usually do the trick. She might pout for a bit but would soon revert to normal. If she had the opportunity to speak to anyone else, however, such as my parents, who we FaceTimed most days, or Andy Clarke, her social worker, it was harder to correct. In fact, I didn't even try, as people tended to find it all too cute, and it felt harsh to step in and reprimand her in front of them.

Still, I knew I had to keep edging her in the right direction; this was a learned behaviour, surely, perhaps born out of a deep-seated desire to return to being a baby, and to get that kind of loving attention from adults – an extreme example of the kind of behaviours often seen in small children when a new baby sibling came along. I knew it could, therefore, be unlearned as well, and also knew the psychologist would probably be able to tell me how to handle it properly. In the meantime, I would just work on experience and instinct, to help her begin to check herself when she was doing it, and to gradually free herself of what had obviously become an instinctive crutch.

The food situation seemed to be calming down too. After two and half weeks Amelie no longer took food from our plates, and though she would still sulk if she saw that we left anything for the composting caddy without offering it to her, it was becoming much less of an issue. (In that regard, I was keen to keep everything on an even keel, anyway, as I knew as much as the next person about how issues around food and body image could so adversely affect a child's well-being in their future life.)

It was no word of a lie then, when Christine called towards the end of the third week about us doing respite, when I told her that Amelie was still being an absolute poppet.

'In fact, she's blossoming,' I enthused. 'Despite all her eccentricities. She's well-behaved, she's always cheerful and she keeps her bedroom like a five-star hotel.'

'Good,' said Christine firmly. A little *too* firmly. 'Because you're going to need all your energies this coming weekend, I have to warn you. Assuming you're still up for helping a fellow foster-carer-in-need? And she really is – the poor woman is at the end of her tether.'

Christine went on to explain that the carer in question, a lady of around my age, who had been fostering on her own since her marriage had ended and her own children had grown up, was currently fostering a young pair of siblings, a two-year-old called Harlan and his eight-month-old baby sister, Layla. 'Both born to a mother who was addicted to heroin,' Christine added, 'and with both suffering quite horrible withdrawal symptoms when they were born.'

My son Tyler – my beloved former foster son, for whom we'd long ago stopped using the term – had been born to a heroin-addicted mother, so this was a circumstance that was particularly close to home. I knew it usually came with significant problems for any child, from obvious birth defects to painful withdrawal symptoms, and behavioural and emotional problems as they grew up. 'Oh, the poor things,' I said, 'and you say they might be problematic? Or is "might be" not quite the right term?'

'Probably not, to be fair,' Christine confirmed. 'Janice – that's their carer – has had them more or less since Layla was born, and she's noticed that Harlan, in particular, isn't anywhere near normal milestones. He doesn't really speak yet, and has only just started walking. He still sleeps in a cot too – he's not really safe to be in a bed yet – and is still, she says, nowhere near being ready to be potty trained. Oh, and apparently they cry an awful lot.'

I was just thinking how abruptly the current peace and quiet was going to disappear, even if only temporarily, when Christine added, 'Though there is one positive. The baby is crawling, which is a good sign that she is meeting at least one important milestone. Though the downside is that Janice says that she's into everything and has to be watched constantly, so I suppose I'm playing fast and loose with the word "positive" as well.'

I couldn't help but laugh. 'You're not a very good saleswoman, Chris,' I told her. 'But I suppose that's not the point. And yes, of course we're still happy to help. Though how long is this short break going to last? Just the weekend?'

'Yes, just the 48 hours,' she said, 'and not a minute longer, I promise. If we're good to go, Jan will drop them off at yours around teatime tomorrow. She won't come in herself, obviously, and you obviously need to keep your distance, but you and Mike can go to her car and get all their things out. Oh, that's a thought. Do you have a cot? Janice will bring along a travel cot for the baby, but I thought you might have one knocking about anyway, for the grandkids? If not, we'll sort one out for you.'

'Don't worry. I have an actual cot,' I said. 'Which sounds as if it might be the better option, given the boy's age. It's dismantled at the moment but since Mike has been on a fix-it mission since lockdown began, he'll soon get it put back together.'

'Brilliant. You are a godsend. Seriously, she is going to be *so* happy. I think they are pretty full-on to care for in normal times, but with lockdown as well, and all her usual family support effectively scotched, it's just so exhausting for her. So just a couple of days and nights to herself will make all the difference, as I'm sure I don't need to tell you.'

She didn't. I'd been there enough times myself. And, as is so often the case, a bit of respite could really work wonders, topping up the emotional tanks and giving you the wherewithal to get stuck back in. And I felt for her. Looking after a toddler and a baby was hard work at the best of times so I didn't doubt she must be struggling. And, well, I thought, as I headed back out into the garden to fill Mike in, it wouldn't hurt to have a couple of hyper-busy days. It was all too easy to get entrenched in doing not terribly much, and being stuck in the house, despite the sunshine, was getting slightly tedious.

As was becoming the case often now, Amelie was more than happy to be Mike's little helper, and was busy offering help and instructions as the hot-tub housing took shape, handing him nails and screws as requested, and unsolicited advice about technique.

'Are we getting our new friends?' she asked excitedly, as I crossed the lawn to fill them in. From the minute I'd mentioned that other children might be coming to us for a sleepover, she'd been busy drawing and colouring in pictures to greet them with and had generally been like a bottle of pop.

'We are indeed,' I confirmed, but before I could go on, she added, 'and are they going to live with us for ever-n-ever-n-ever?'

Since she'd run across, arms outstretched, I squatted down on the grass for a hug. 'No, sweetie,' I reminded her. 'Just for the weekend. For two days. Remember? But it'll be fun, won't it? And I'm sure the older one, who is a little boy called Harlan, will be very happy to have you play some nice games with him.'

I actually had no such idea, but I didn't doubt that Amelie would enjoy keeping him occupied, whatever stage of development he was at. I'd yet to see her interact with any other children, obviously, but, going by the way she'd been since she'd arrived with us, my hunch was that she'd be like a regular mother hen.

'And the other one?' Mike asked.

'An eight-month-old baby. Called Layla.'

'A baby?' Amelie did a little skip. 'Oh, I *love* babies!'

'Me too,' I said. 'We're going to have a fun weekend, aren't we? Oh,' I added, turning to Mike, 'we're going to need to reassemble our cot. They'll bring a travel cot for the little one, but the boy's still in a cot too, apparently, so I said we could use ours, and –'

'That'll be the royal "we" then, will it?' he said, grinning at Amelie. 'Though where were you planning on putting them? Ty's room? Be a bit of a squeeze in there with two cots.'

He was right, of course. Though Tyler had moved out a while back – in fact, had never actually lived in our current house, having moved away to live with his girlfriend before we moved ourselves – I had pretty much moved his old bedroom with us, wholesale. Which did make sense. Since our other kids and grandkids all lived very locally, it was always Tyler and Naomi who used it when they came to stay anyway. Plus, at some point, if and when they moved somewhere more permanently, presumably once she'd finished college, he'd no doubt be glad to be reunited with all his stuff. Though, in the meantime, it did double duty as what Mike called my 'staging post', the place where stuff without a destination yet usually migrated to – bags of old bedding, old toys, clothes due to be sold or recycled, books and DVDs – anything, in fact, that was on its way *somewhere* – but just not quite yet. And that included the disassembled cot. So yes, Mike was right. It definitely would be a squash.

That said, though, it made more sense to have the baby in with us, and just set up Harlan in Ty's room. I didn't know the dynamic between the siblings, but one thing I did know was that leaving an unknown toddler and baby unsupervised together was a recipe for stress and misadventure – and that applied at any hour of the day or night. I said so.

Mike frowned. 'So, we're talking night feeds still, are we?'

At which Amelie tugged at my top. 'I can feed the baby!' she chirruped. 'I'm good at feeding babies! The baby can come in my room. They can *both* come in my room! We can have a tea party and play schools and do hide and seek and all sorts of fun things!'

'I imagine you could, kiddo,' Mike said, 'but I'm afraid we can't have them sleeping in your bedroom. You can play in there with them but come bedtime, they need to be safely in their cots, and in their own rooms. Not least –' he added, as she opened her mouth to object – 'because you, because *all* of us, will need our beauty sleep, and if they're in with you, they'll be having *way* too much fun. Anyway, I'd better down tools, eh? And get this cot all set up. Wanna help?'

He didn't even need to ask, obviously. 'And then I'll make them some name badges,' Amelie said, 'and get them both some teddies, and we can make a plan for the lessons for when we play schools, and then, before they get here, we can –'

'Erm …' Mike said, chuckling, 'pause for breath, by any chance?'

She was still chattering away as she followed him back inside to get the cot set up. Whatever else was true, one thing was, I felt certain. That our new visitors would likely not know what had hit them …

# Chapter 6

By the time the siblings arrived the following afternoon, Amelie was almost bursting with excited anticipation. It wasn't just like the annoying 'Are we there yet?' that all parents are used to on long car journeys. No, this was way off that scale. Up until this point the only evidence I'd seen of how controlling Amelie was of her immediate environment had been the bedroom-cleaning routine which was still very much part of her day, and the way she would get upset if she got anything at all wrong on the educational games Mike had installed on her tablet. She seemed to hate to ask for help, tending towards the 'Me do it! Me do it!' that I was more used to seeing in toddlers, and if there was a problem or puzzle she couldn't solve herself she would be more likely to throw the tablet down in frustration and demand that Mike remove the game than ask for or accept any help or guidance.

We would try our best, of course, to get her to allow us to show her how the problem could be solved, or, if she was determined to solve it without help, to suggest that, rather than give up, she keep on trying. It would usually fall on deaf ears, though, and if we did manage to persuade her, it would be no time at all before she grew so frustrated again that she could barely see the screen for angry tears. It was sad to see, because it seemed the only negative emotions she displayed were anger and frustration at herself. Another manifestation of her erratic parenting? I could only imagine so.

Right now, however, with our new visitors imminent, I was starting to see another aspect to Amelie's psyche: just how obsessive she could be about what was happening and when. It was another piece of a clearly very complicated jigsaw.

'Tell me again, Casey,' she said at breakfast, 'what will Harlan say when he sees me? What will baby Layla do? How long till they get here?'

It was no good, I was learning, to respond with 'I don't know'. I always had to put forward my best guess. I'd also had recent experience of this kind of thing; our last foster child, Ethan, had been obsessive about timings, and I had learned not to go down that particular route, as he really struggled if he didn't have something definite to latch on to. Ethan's issues had also been related to control. He'd come to us after his mother's tragic death due to a heroin overdose and, a regular user in the months leading up to her death, she would set a timer on his iPad when she went next door to the neighbours to do drugs, so he'd know not to worry, because he knew when to expect her home again. Which, by any yardstick, was a tragedy in itself. And he'd been even younger than Amelie.

I could only make an educated guess about the root of Amelie's own concern about the nature of upcoming events, but it seemed a good rule of thumb just to run with it. 'I imagine it shouldn't be too much longer till they get here,' I said, smiling, 'and, like I said before, little Harlan can't speak very well, and the baby can't speak at all, so I bet they will just smile at you and maybe make some happy sounds so that you know they like you very much.'

Amelie looked down at the pink and orange gingham summer dress she'd selected to wear, and frowned. 'I'm going to go get changed, Casey,' she said. 'I don't think the twins are going to like what I'm wearing.'

It was my turn to frown. 'The twins? They're not twins, sweetie. They're a brother and baby sister. And why ever not? That dress is beautiful. I'd stay just as you are.'

'No. They're *my* twins,' Amelie said, surprising me with the slight note of vehemence in her voice. 'I told all my babies upstairs that the twins are coming, and they have to be *very* nice to them, but I just remembered, I've made their favourite colour on their school badges and it's blue. So I need to find something *blue*.'

So that was me told. And there seemed little point in fighting that battle, so I told her we could go upstairs and choose something else for her to wear. At least it would while away a bit more time. Thankfully, among the various items of clothing currently neatly folded in her chest of drawers were a pair of denim shorts and a pretty blue and white spotted T-shirt, and after a very tiring two hours of placating her when she got upset about how long we had been waiting, we were finally at the door, ready to greet our new houseguests.

Jan (Janice) was out of the car by the time we'd opened the front door and, having opened one of the back passenger doors and the boot, was currently fixing a mask over her face. She then began unpacking various items from the boot, while a plaintive whine could be heard from inside the car.

I felt a bit useless, having to stand there watching from my step, but Christine had told me it was okay to help her, hadn't she? Just as long as everyone involved got masked up and we didn't get too close to one another. Though I was also aware that I'd probably set curtains twitching; there was this creeping sense of people watching other people's behaviour, keeping an eye on anyone who dared break the strict social distancing and 'stay at home' rules. 'Don't worry – I'll brave it,' Mike said, having come through to join us and already masked up, clearly having already read my thoughts.

'Me too!' Amelie trilled, making a break to go and follow him. 'No, sweetie,' I said, pulling her back again. 'You wait with me. Remember how we all have to stay safe?'

'But we *are* safe,' she complained.

'Yes, indeed we are,' I agreed. 'But remember the nasty virus that's going around? We need to keep our distance so we can't pass it on to one another, remember?'

'But you said I could play with Harlan and Layla,' she pointed out.

'Yes, you can – we *all* can – once we're all inside. But the grown-ups have to be careful, because if the grown-ups get the virus they could be very, very poorly, and –'

'Hey, twins!' she yelled over me, waving her arm around madly. 'Hey, twins! We're safe! Come and play!'

She was bellowing so loud I wouldn't have been surprised if half the neighbours had come out. 'Goodness me!' I said. 'Calm down, love. They'll be coming in a minute. Look,' I added, 'Mike has to help get all their things in first, doesn't he?' And what a lot of it there seemed to be too. There was the travel cot, a couple of ride-on toys, various bags and a couple of boxes. There was even a double buggy.

'Well,' Jan said sheepishly, as she handed the latter over the invisible two-metre airlock, 'I wasn't going to bother but then I thought – you might like to take them out.' She grinned at me. 'For sanity reasons mostly.' She also handed over the temporary care plan and a couple of pages of helpful handwritten information, then, while Mike brought the last of the children's belongings in, went back to get the children themselves out of the car, while Amelie hopped excitedly from foot to foot on the front doorstep, anxious to get a glimpse of her new playmates.

# Little Girl Lost

The baby was sound asleep when Jan set her down in her car seat, and looking as all babies do when they are sleeping – as if the proverbial butter wouldn't melt. And as I'd yet to meet a baby I didn't want to cuddle, I was happy to take her and drink in her delicious baby-scent.

The little lad, on the other hand, had an odd air about him – not anxious, not hostile, not anything really. As if he was not really with us, but lost in a world of his own. His only action, as he stood there, his hand clasped by Jan, was to pull his other one away sharply as soon as Amelie tried to grasp it.

'I can't stay,' Jan said, 'because I also have a 17-year-old in my care now.'

'Oh, my lord – I didn't realise.'

'Oh, it's fine. He's not that much of a challenge, very sweet lad, actually, but he *is* a teenager and we *are* in the middle of a pandemic, and I daren't leave him home alone for too long. You know what they're like at that age, even at the best of times; he'll be off given half a chance. And so would I have been at that age, bless him, if I were under house arrest. It's so tough on the young people, isn't it? Anyway, it'll have to be a quick hello–goodbye, I'm afraid. Mind you,' she added, the corners of her eyes crinkling in amusement, 'it's not as if I'm allowed to stay anyway, is it?'

I nodded. What a woman. She really was having to multitask. And on her own too. No wonder she was craving a bit of respite. 'Good point. Off you go,' I said, shooing her off down the path. 'And I hope you manage to at least get *some* rest.'

'Two nights' unbroken sleep. That'll be the main thing, and I'm so looking forward to it.' Then she laughed. 'Not that I want to be a harbinger of doom, obviously. And you never know. They might be perfect angels for you. So often the way, isn't it?'

'It's *fine*,' I reassured her. 'You get off. Enjoy the respite.'

She didn't need any further encouragement; she was back into her car in a matter of moments. 'Call me if anything crops up!' she called as she switched on the engine.

I stuck a thumb up but, of course, I wouldn't. Well, not unless there was something I *seriously* needed advice with. That was, after all, the unspoken pact. And how hard could 48 hours with these two little ones be? The baby currently in my arms was, well, just a baby, and I was a match for any two-year-old, however much of the proverbial tiny emperor he turned out to be.

And Harlan definitely seemed to be that. I noticed that when Jan had kissed him goodbye and given him a parting hug, he showed as much reaction as, well, as a plank of wood. And as soon as I ushered him over the threshold, he ambled off down the hallway as if not even noticing we were there, let alone that he was in a completely unfamiliar place.

'Well, this should be fun,' Mike remarked drily as we watched him toddle off.

'I don't think so. He doesn't want to be my friend,' Amelie said.

'Oh, I'm sure he will, love,' I said, as we followed him down the hall. 'It's all just a bit new for him, that's all.'

'I don't care *anyway*,' she said, with a huff. 'I can play with the baby. And *he* can go and play by himself.'

Remembering the warning about Layla being able to crawl, I eschewed putting her on the sofa, even though she was still deeply asleep, and instead made a well in one of our large bean bags with my foot and settled her into that instead.

'Yes, I know you want to play, love,' I told Amelie firmly, 'but babies need their sleep so you'll have to wait till she wakes up.'

In response, she duly sat down cross-legged on the floor in front of her to do just that, having clearly decided Harlan was now *persona non grata*. And by now, the boy himself, having presumably not realised the large bifold doors into the garden were open, had made his way into the utility room and was banging on the side door, as if hoping to be allowed to go outside. Mike got to him first, and attempted to coax him away, trying to take his hand to guide him back into the main living room. 'Come on, little man,' he said, 'let's go see what toys you've brought to play with, shall we? I'm sure there must be lots in those big bags you came with.'

Harlan, in reply, simply turned to stare at Mike, his expression vacant and then, without his blank expression even changing one iota, let out the most ear-piercing scream I had heard in a very long time.

Mike and I were stunned into an open-mouthed silence. Amelie, however, was not. 'Ouuuuuch! That *hurts*!' she yelled angrily from the sitting area, cupping her hands over her ears. 'You just stop that, RIGHT NOW, young man!'

While Mike and exchanged glances – where had *that* bellow come from? – Harlan blinked and only screamed all the louder.

I glanced back towards the living room and, entirely as I had expected, Layla had now woken up. Though not in a state of distress, as we might have assumed. No, she merely looked around her, as if taking her new surroundings in, then tried to wriggle and roll her way off the bean bag. Leaving Mike to deal with Harlan, and with Amelie still cupping her ears, I approached the baby, who had now manoeuvred herself into a sitting position on the floor.

Not for long, however. I was going to scoop her up, but she was already eyeing up the coffee table, and had soon shuffled over, reached up and pulled herself to a standing position, then, while I waited to see what she could do, let go and proceeded to make a couple of tottering steps towards me. She then faltered and began to fall, at which point I caught her, but not before I had taken in her highly unusual way of 'walking'.

I'd never seen anything like it. I was already pretty shocked that a child so young *could* walk, but the way she did so was really bizarre, because she wasn't walking on her soles. In fact, her ankles were so turned over, that she was virtually walking on the insteps; sort of inwards, but a lot further than that, so that she was almost walking using the tops of her feet. Which must have hurt, surely?

There was no indication that it was doing so, however. Was there some sort of birth deformity involved? The child herself, however, couldn't seem to care less. In fact, Layla's response to my scooping her up was to lean her head into my chest, and, with one hot little arm clamped around my neck, to start sucking loudly and contentedly on her thumb.

For whatever reason, this seemed to galvanise Harlan. He stopped screaming abruptly, and, having marched straight across the room to me, started tugging on his little sister's dangling feet.

'Mamma! Mamma!' he yelled, glaring up angrily at me, and tugging ever harder on his sister.

This, in turn, seemed to galvanise Amelie. 'Woah there, young man!' she shouted, and before either Mike or I could stop her, she grabbed a handful of Harlan's hair and started pulling it. 'I'mma gonna knock the bloody devil right out of you if you don't stop that nonsense!' she shouted at him.

'Fun?' I mouthed at Mike as he came to the rescue. Five minutes in and we were already in a state of utter mayhem. What with Harlan yanking on the baby's foot, and Amelie yanking on Harlan's hair, it was as if we were suddenly in charge of a single, shouting, screaming, totally out-of-control organism, to which the baby was contributing by kicking out both her legs and, for good measure, now holding a fistful of my own hair. Though, to be fair, at least she wasn't contributing to the noise levels, as her free thumb was still firmly in her mouth.

It took a while for Mike to prise Harlan's hand from his little sister's ankle, while I attempted to do similarly with Amelie's grip on Harlan's hair.

'Amelie!' I said once I had her hand gripped in my own. 'You mustn't do that, do you hear? You can't hurt people like that – especially someone so much smaller than you are. Look, you've made him cry now, see?'

Amelie looked at Harlan, whose screams had indeed now turned to sobs. But if I thought she'd be contrite, I was mistaken. '*Okay* then,' she said grudgingly. 'I'm *sorry*' – which she clearly wasn't – 'but this lady is not your mamma, and stop your bloody *screaming*!'

Where *had* this all come from? I was totally aghast. Harlan was really crying now, big tears falling down his cheeks as he looked, wide-eyed, at this furious red-cheeked child who was yelling at him. He then threw himself against me, and held both arms aloft. 'Mamma,' he sobbed, 'Mamma!', while stretching his arms up, obviously desperate to be picked up. Mike duly did pick him up and snuggled him against his chest. 'It's okay, little man,' he soothed. 'Shhhh … It's okay.'

It was an action that clearly displeased Amelie, who now whirled around and threw herself down on the sofa. 'I don't *want* you,' she barked. 'And I don't want him *either*!' She then reached for her tablet, flipped the cover, and switched it on, pointedly turning her whole body away from us, and leaving the two of us, one apiece, holding the babies.

'I think we need to make a plan,' Mike said, over the top of Harlan's head.

Within a couple of hours, it had become clear that we needed not only a plan, but some way of physically restraining our three little ones, it soon becoming clear that to have all three in the same space was likely to be a recipe for further outbreaks of chaos, and that Harlan, in particular, was a law unto himself, tending to wander off whenever the mood took him. I therefore dispatched Mike to drive to our daughter Riley's house to borrow a couple of extra safety gates. We'd already put one up in the entrance to what was going to be Harlan's bedroom, but we also needed one for the doorway from the living area to the hallway, and another for the door into the utility room, the appliances and cupboards in which seemed to hold great appeal. And while he was gone, I did my best to referee.

By the time Mike was back, I had already established three things. That 'Mamma' appeared to be the only word Harlan spoke and, if he shouted that, I had to get to him in double quick time or he would lash out at Layla. In contrast, Layla seemed to exist in a state of perpetual bliss. I didn't once hear her cry, despite her ambling around and falling over often – it simply didn't seem to bother her. She would simply huff and puff a bit, then pull herself back up, and set off again, cruising round the room. If Harlan hit, kicked or pushed her, which he did any time she entered his orbit, she would just look at him as if confused then carry on in her own little world. And despite all of Amelie's plans to play schools or mummies and daddies with these new children, rather than fill her with the happiness she'd envisaged, their presence – Harlan's particularly – was clearly causing her no end of torment.

'That child is driving me *crazy*!' she exploded at him the minute he reappeared. 'Look!' she added, jabbing a finger in Harlan's direction as, for the umpteenth time, he was pushing his sister over. 'You!' she raged. 'You little devil! Just you wait! The FBI are going to come for you in the *middle of the night*! And take you away and to do speriments on you! You little bugger!'

It was, fair to say, somewhat stressful. Even leaving aside Amelie's frequent angry outbursts, these two little ones were exhausting. How did Jan cope with the two of them day after day? No wonder the teen she had in with her sought escape at every opportunity. Pandemic or no pandemic, I didn't doubt my own would have as well. And no wonder Jan had skipped away with such a spring in her step. No wonder she was at the end of her tether.

For Mike and I, however, as we kept reminding one another, it was only going to be for two days. And as bedtime approached, things did calm down a bit, especially when I announced that I'd be putting Harlan to bed first, which, in Amelie's case, provoked a heart-felt 'Good!'

Taking him up to bed, however, was not the same as getting him down, which took me the best part of an hour and a half. So much for the idea of him sleeping in a cot so he wouldn't fall out of bed; he was like a squirrel monkey; he could scale the cot side in seconds and didn't seem to care that he then landed on the carpet from a great height. He simply would not stay put. I told him stories, I stroked his head, I sang to him, I hummed at him. I went through my entire repertoire of lullabies and old sixties ballads twice. But every time he nodded off and I tiptoed away, his eyes would ping open, he'd do a Fosbury flop over his prison bars and run to the safety gate, then shake the bars angrily and scream, 'Mamma, Mamma, Mamma!'

It took five or six rounds of this before I could finally return downstairs, by which time not only were Amelie and Layla both asleep, but Mike, the latter sweetly snuggled up against his chest, was softly snoring as well.

For a moment or two I seriously considered joining them. Fortunately however, getting Layla down was easy. I simply prised her off Mike, and, after checking her nappy, took her straight upstairs and laid her in the cot in our room, during which at no point did she even really stir. And though Amelie put up a small show of defiance about not being allowed to have the baby in with her, I think she was too exhausted to argue for long, and by nine we had the house – and some blissful silence – to ourselves.

Not that we could really enjoy it. We were both pretty shattered and went up soon after, all too aware that Jan's notes included the ominous words, 'They generally wake up around 5 a.m.'

We therefore crept into our bedroom like two particularly nervous mice, and undressed both carefully and wordlessly. It was almost completely dark, but as I tiptoed round to my side of the bed, there was enough light to notice the outline of the baby in her cot.

I beckoned Mike to come see. 'Look,' I whispered. 'Look what Layla's doing.'

It was one of the strangest things I'd seen. She had found her night-time bottle and was drinking from it, half awake and half asleep, but, curiously, she wasn't using her hands to hold the bottle. Instead she had it firmly gripped between her feet. Her hands, meanwhile, were both above her head, and she was soothing herself by playing with her hair.

'Well, she clearly knows what she's doing,' Mike whispered. 'Come on. Leave her to it and let's try to get some sleep.'

I didn't need any encouragement; I was asleep within moments. But come the early hours, the smallest of sounds woke me up – though, given that there was a baby in the room with us, that was entirely as I'd expected. When I opened my eyes, however, I could immediately see, even in the gloom, that Layla was still sound asleep. So what had made me stir? That long-honed maternal instinct to anticipate a baby's imminent waking? Pushing myself up a little and leaning out, I silently watched her for a few moments, and it was only then that I became aware of a dark form on the carpet beside the cot, which, as my eyes adjusted, began to resolve itself. And into the form of Amelie, curled up on the floor beside the cot, using one of the cushions Mike had jettisoned from our bed as a pillow.

She looked so peaceful that for a moment or two I considered leaving her as she was. But she had no blanket and would surely soon feel the cold. Plus, if and when Layla did wake up, she obviously would wake up too, potentially adding a layer of complication to what I obviously hoped would be a simple business of soothing the baby straight back to sleep.

So I slipped out of bed, went across, and placed a hand on her back. 'Sweetie,' I whispered, as she immediately jerked awake, 'we need to get you back into your bed.'

She shook her head immediately she came to. 'I have to stay here,' she answered, keeping her voice very low, as I had. 'I need to keep a watch over baby Layla.'

'She's fine,' I whispered back. 'Mike and I are here with her. And you'll get cold lying there with no covers to keep you warm. Come on. Let's get you back to bed.'

'*Please*,' she begged. 'I'm not cold. I want to stay here, so I know she's safe.'

'She *is* safe,' I said. 'She's fine. Look, she's fast asleep and dreaming.' Though she wouldn't be for much longer if we kept this whispered conversation up. 'Come on, sweetie,' I urged, rubbing Amelie's shoulder, 'let's get you back to your bedroom.'

'But if I go, she might be *stolen*,' she hissed.

'Stolen?' This was taking concern for the baby's welfare to a whole other level.

'Yes,' she insisted, 'be stolen. Like my *twins* were!'

I let Amelie stay, in the end. It was already gone four, after all. Tucked her up where she was with the throw from the end of our bed. Twins though? Twins that were stolen? What twins was she talking about? Her mother's? Did she have, or had she had, siblings? I tried to rationalise it away as just another of her mother's mental-illness related fantasies. But to weave a tale in which two little ones had been taken away under their noses? That seemed particularly close to the bone. Had they been real, in fact? Had her mum *actually* had two babies taken into care? And could the loss of those babies have compounded her mental health difficulties? But if that *were* true, surely someone would know. How could something so devastating remain unknown to everyone who was dealing with her now?

Which was, to be fair, a very naive question. Which I was still pondering 45 minutes later when, right on cue, I heard a bellow from the next-door bedroom. 'Mammmmmma!!!!'

# Chapter 7

With the following day proving to be a re-run of the first, there was no opportunity to glean any further information from Amelie about her own 'stolen' twins. Not that I'd intended to press her on the matter. I would simply be alert to anything further on the mystery being said. Which it wasn't, perhaps not least because the following evening I pre-empted her desire to sleep on the floor beside Layla by, despite Mike's fruitless eye-rolling and tutting, making up a little bed for her on our bedroom floor.

Besides, it could wait. I would record it in my log and, when the opportunity arose, ask Christine if she could find out anything further. It could wait anyway; between the three of them they ran us pretty ragged, what with Layla's seeming death wish around the furniture, Harlan's intermittent screaming and Amelie's irritation around the latter, causing her to shout at him incessantly, it was all Mike and I could do to keep on top of things. I could only console myself with the thought that it would be over before we knew it, and then felt guilty about our poor fellow carer as a consequence.

By the time Jan came to pick her charges up, we couldn't lie. We were frazzled and exhausted. So much so that, immediately she arrived, Jan could see it in my face. 'Uh-oh,' she said, as she stopped the requisite two metres from our open doorway, 'were they as challenging as billed? I almost feel guilty now that I'm feeling so bright-eyed and refreshed.'

I couldn't help but laugh. 'I've been feeling guilty too,' I admitted. 'Like a grandparent jibing that at least they can give them back. But I'm happy that you're happy. I take it you made the most of it? Well, as far as you were able to in this bloody lockdown.'

'Oh, it was bliss,' she said. 'Just things like soaking in the bath. And my teen, bless him – it was as if all his Christmasses had come at once. He didn't even so much as whine about escaping. It's been a real shot in the arm for both of us, this break. We even did a jigsaw together. And if you'd told me *that* would happen a month ago, I'd have said you were stark staring potty!'

'Good,' I said. 'And no two ways about it – I can see why you needed one.'

Jan nodded. 'Amazing how being confined to barracks makes a week seem like a lifetime, isn't it? They actually weren't half as challenging before this – mostly down to the fact that they were both at a day nursery, so I had regular time each day to recharge. And their granny and gramps, too. There was regular contact there too, but, of course, that's all out the proverbial window for now. Ah –' she added, glancing behind me. 'Is that a small whirlwind I hear approaching?'

'Sounds like it,' I agreed, as Mike came to join us, Layla in his arms and Harlan ambling along beside him, having been herded back in from the garden while I answered the door. No sign of Amelie, however. They had delighted her enough. Despite her night vigils, she had already announced, with some feeling, that it was 'definitely time for the twins to go home now'.

Indeed, when Mike and I reappeared in the living room, having seen everyone off, she made no bones about her relief at their departure. '*Finally*,' she said, making a big deal of putting down her tablet, where she'd been watching cartoons, 'some peace and bloody quiet around here!'

My response was automatic. 'Amelie, remember the rules about using words like that?' But even as I said it, I knew it would fall on deaf ears. Amelie didn't swear either for impact or for shock value, or to try and gain adult attention. She merely trotted out phrases she obviously heard regularly. It would require a systematic intervention to change that behaviour, one I didn't feel she was ready for as yet. It was another of the things I'd be discussing with the psychologist. In the meantime, I could only silently concur. The peace and bloody quiet were bloody lovely.

And lasted all of 20 minutes. Amelie's chattering – sometimes nonsensical, sometimes contradictory, but always intriguing – soon started up again. 'I miss having my friends now,' she announced, while helping me clear the mess of toys away.

'Oh, really?' Mike said, chuckling. 'Not half an hour back you couldn't wait to see them gone.'

'Not *really*,' she said, as if she hadn't spent the last 48 hours shouting at them to make them stop – er – shouting, or was now in the midst of a period of remorse that she hadn't quite appreciated their presence enough. 'They were friends and I'm never allowed friends. Not in the house.'

'And why was that, lovely?' I asked, already anticipating the answer. Which duly came.

'Because the bad mens from the FBI might poison them.'

'And why do you think they would have done that?' I couldn't help myself asking.

'You *know*,' she said. 'Because they are a big gang of evil monsters, and they are always listening to us and watching us. *Always*. But they can come here,' she said, pausing in her re-stacking of some beakers, 'because it's safe here. Can you ask the lady? Can they come back tomorrow?'

'Perhaps they will come back,' I told her. 'Though definitely not tomorrow.'

'But soon?'

'Perhaps,' I said again. Though definitely not *too*

84

soon, Mike's and my eyes said to each other's. We'd need at least another couple of days, I reckoned, to get over the last 48 hours. A chance to reconnect with our mostly peaceful non-routine routine.

Indeed, so anxious was I about another frenetic respite placement that when I saw Christine's name pop up on my phone display a couple of days later, I hardly dared answer it in case she was going to ask me to have Harlan and Layla again the following weekend. I said as much when I finally picked up.

'No,' Christine said, laughing, 'well, not so soon anyhow. I did see the emphatic note on your sheets about needing a 48-hour respite of your own.'

'Was it that obvious?' I said. 'Though to be honest, what with the lack of sleep and the constant three-way fire-fighting, it was pretty exhausting. Which isn't to say we wouldn't be happy to have them over again if need be. Ideally, though, just not *yet*.'

'Don't worry,' Christine reassured me, 'Jan's back firing on all cylinders. And don't forget, she doesn't have another little one in the mix. From your log it sounds as if the dynamics between the three of them were a big part of what made it so challenging. Amelie clearly isn't used to having other little ones around her, is she? Oh, and in answer to the question you raised about other children going into care, I've done a bit of digging and I can't enlighten you further, I'm afraid. There's nothing to hint at that scenario in Kelly's notes. It's possible, obviously, because we're not remotely joined up, as you know; if she has history with social services in another part of the country, we're not aware of it, but that doesn't mean that's not the case. We're obviously not privy to Mum's entire medical history, either, so it's possible she lost a baby – or indeed twin babies – at some point.'

'I did wonder about that,' I said. 'It would seem to fit, don't you think? I mean I can only surmise about the effect on Mum's mental health, or if it was something like that which caused her mental health to deteriorate – God knows, if it *did* happen, it must have been appalling. Beyond wretched. But I just have this sense that there must be a thread of truth in there somewhere for Amelie to have used the term "twins" the way she did. Though she's not mentioned it again, and I'm not about to start sleuthing. It seems to me to be something for the psychologist to explore.'

'Exactly,' Christine said, 'and that's partly why I'm phoning. I have a couple of bits of good news, in fact.'

Christine went on to explain that the ELAC worker had been in touch with our local primary school and they would be willing to take Amelie on a temporary basis, for a full week of half days, or three full days a week. 'Whichever fits in with you and Mike best. Though it'll be a couple of weeks or so before she can start,' she continued, 'because they're working with only a skeleton staff and because of all the new protocols can only take a limited number of children at a time. So what they're doing is working on a rotation.

'Obviously all the key workers' children are in full time, but others, like Amelie, and the kids with special educational needs, get a few weeks at a time, and then they are taken out for a few weeks while others on the waiting list get the opportunity. It's not ideal, I know, but it's better than nothing, isn't it? And, in the meantime, they are happy to send through some bits of work to your email for Amelie, which might be a help if you're struggling to get her to do anything productive.'

I explained that that wasn't really an issue. 'In that respect,' I told Christine, 'Amelie really is a model child. She's happy to tackle pretty much any task I set her. It's all the other stuff I'm worried about – like how she's fallen hook, line and sinker for all her mother's conspiracy theories. She's clearly had all kinds of nonsense drilled into her for years, and I'm not sure how to tackle it. To be honest, I'm not even sure if I *should* try. I'm also still really concerned about her attachment issues; it's as if you could plonk her down anywhere and she'd simply get on with it. It's deeply unsettling – and a bit of a new one on me – to be caring for a child who's really not exhibiting any of the behaviours you'd expect. That lack of distress, of acting out, of taking us on – all that kind of stuff I'm used to. It's … well, the very fact that she causes so few upsets, I find that worrying in itself. Apart from the way she tries to control her environment – still very much a thing, by the way; I think her issue with poor little Harlan was down to that – she doesn't seem to worry about a thing, and that's precisely what's going to make her so vulnerable.'

'I hear you,' Christine said. 'And that's my other bit of news. If you can organise for Amelie to be busy tomorrow morning, the psychologist can speak to you via Teams at 10.00 a.m. She will send you a link to your email and you guys can have a virtual face-to-face for half an hour. Obviously you'll have to find a quiet place to speak, away from little ears.'

'Oh, there's no problem there,' I said. 'I can do it in our snug while Amelie plays builder's mate out in the garden with Mike.'

I crossed my fingers tightly as I hung up. Good weather and good moods permitting, that was. And what was going on with the weather right now? When was the last time it had been so relentlessly sunny? Which was great, of course, because I did love my sunshine. But we were surely, surely due to see some rain ...

As it turned out, on Thursday morning, the sun came out as usual, and when I was setting up for my Teams meeting, Amelie was employed more as apprentice to Mike's head gardener, as some delay in some part or other of the hot-tub area project meant another project being tackled: pricking out tomato plants and dealing with the copious amounts of weeds the enduring good weather had inspired to run rampant.

With them both safely occupied, I settled down in our 'snug' with my laptop, and logged on to see the smiling face of a woman who looked to be in her thirties, and who seemed to be in a similarly domestic setting. It felt odd getting such an intimate glimpse of what looked like her master bedroom; I could see the edge of a white-painted iron bedstead, and some kind of poster on the wall that looked as if it might be from a theatre. Adjacent to that was a high shelf – one of those ones you use to prop pictures on – and which held photographs, a slender candle and a trio of greenish glass jars containing dried flowers. There was also a string of heart-shaped fairy lights threaded through everything, and though they weren't switched on, I could imagine the room as if they were, bathing it in a gentle romantic light. Such a personal space. I felt almost like an intruder. Though I soon remembered that my own home was open to all-comers, and always had been. So many professional conversations had been and always would be conducted around my dining table. So many social workers, small hands clutched nervously in theirs, had trooped up and down my stairs over the years. I felt a kind of pride that I hadn't thought to 'curate my backdrop', as, only half an hour earlier, Riley had commented was now very much 'the thing', saying I also needed to get myself something called a 'ring light'. And given by the attractive glow that was on the woman's face, I suspected she might have. Well, she'd just have to take me as she found me.

The woman waved. 'Amanda Brady,' she said. 'Hello! And please don't be worried. I like to keep things informal.' She smiled then. 'Little choice currently,' she added, as if having read my thoughts. 'It'll be a miracle if one of my kids doesn't invade before we're finished, for which I apologise in advance. Weird times, eh?'

I nodded. 'Weird times indeed. So …' I faltered then, unsure of the agenda. 'How do these things tend to work?'

'Well, this is essentially an exploratory meeting,' she said, gathering some out-of-view paperwork. 'I've read all your reports and the background Christine Bolton provided me with – and that's for both Amelie and her mum. So why don't we start by you outlining where you are, what your immediate concerns are and what you're hoping to achieve? Because from what I've read,' she added, smiling, 'you're doing a grand job so far.'

I glanced down at my notebook, which I'd annotated in readiness. 'Well, I'm concerned that Amelie doesn't appear to miss her mum – not in any way. She barely speaks about her at all, in fact. The only time she mentions her is if she feels she needs to warn me about some perceived danger, such as bugs in computers or the FBI – I'm sure you've read all this already in the notes – and how they implant listening devices and so on. The fire too. I mean, that must have been *deeply* traumatic, but she hasn't mentioned it, not even once. Do I broach these things with her? That's the kind of thing I'm unsure of.'

Amanda Brady was making notes, and was nodding rather than answering, so I felt I might as well press on.

'I mean, at this point I have no idea how long this place-ment is going to be, obviously, but if it's going to be long-term, I just feel I should be doing something, you know? I mean the fact that Amelie seems not to miss Mum one iota rings alarm bells – it's as if I'm fiddling while Rome burns, so to speak – waiting for a psycho-logical meltdown that must surely be coming.'

Amanda put her pen down. 'I'm not sure it will be,' she said. 'From what I can gather, Casey, Amelie's mum, although she *was* around, wasn't fully present. In most cases, as you know, a mother is the centre of a child's universe, but in this case, it seems that Amelie didn't have that anchor. Her mum was so wrapped up in her own turmoil and fragile mental health that Amelie was simply another item in her orbit, so there was no way she could be any kind of rock or lifeline to her daughter. Amelie would have "got" this this from a very early age, so vital connections weren't made, and, sadly, that's stunted her ability to form any emotional attachments.'

Sad, indeed. And how did anyone start to fix it? I'd had lots of kids with the ubiquitous label of 'attachment issues' and in my experience their outcomes weren't great. How on earth did one begin to try and fix that?

But Amanda was carrying straight on. 'As for the fire,' she said, 'let's not forget that Amelie would have led her mother out of that house for all kinds of, to her mind, quite logical reasons. To escape FBI spies, harm-ful rays, poisonous substances and so on, so the fire that night might have been just another of those occasions for Amelie, so perhaps the very real peril might not even have entered her head. It's possible it wasn't the first time her mother had started a fire, don't forget, or covered the windows with foil to escape detection. In fact, I would venture to guess that if you *did* bring it up, the child would be very matter-of-fact about it.'

I nodded. This too made sense. 'So how can I help, then?' I asked.

'There is no magic wand,' Amanda said. 'And in saying so I suspect I'm preaching to the converted. You'll have been here many times before, I'm sure. In fact, it looks like you're already doing everything I would suggest. Modelling normal family behaviour, answering Amelie's questions as far as you are able, gently dissuading her from, or reframing, any outlandish suggestions. There would have been periods in her life when Mum was taking her meds and was relatively stable, so memories of living in a relatively normal environment are still in there somewhere, I'm guessing. The hope has to be that with a prolonged period away from the chaos, Amelie will start to re-make those connections and see her mother's illness for what it is. She's too young for that right now, but that time will eventually come and in the meantime it's never too early to start explaining things to her.'

Amanda went on to suggest that when Amelie mentioned things like the FBI or spies, for example, rather than just ignore what she said and change the subject, I should straight away explain to her, in a child-friendly way, what the FBI organisation actually did for a living, and how they were there to protect citizens, like her and her mum, from harm. 'It's the same principle,' she added, 'if she speaks about checking for poisons, etc. I should tell her about how rigorously all consumables are checked for our safety before anyone buys them. Ditto why security cameras are there.'

I also told Amanda about Amelie's baby behaviours, her eating habits, her need for tidiness and order. And Amanda returned to a period, hypothetical though it was, when Amelie's mum might have been on her meds and relatively stable, and potentially with the supervision and support of a team of health visitors, etc., at a crucial time in Amelie's emotional development. 'At this point,' she explained, 'if we assume Mum was stable and lucid, she would have been desperate to stay on an even keel, and so not risk any chance of losing her daughter. Who wouldn't? This might explain Amelie's regression to a time when she did feel Mum represented security. She might have learned that exhibiting toddler-type behaviour equals care. That regressing to a time when she felt safe and loved is a way to gain positive attention. That in order to make others happy – because she remembers her mum caring about her then perhaps – she sometimes reverts back to that behaviour. It's probably unconscious. I wouldn't be surprised if she doesn't realise she's even doing it.'

'It certainly feels that way,' I said. 'And there doesn't seem to be a pattern. And perhaps the obsession with tidying her bedroom is similarly rooted in that period,' I added, warming to the theme now. 'I wonder if it's because Mum had to "put on a show"; persuade her health visitor that she really was on top of things by making sure the house was immaculate and squeaky clean. And would perhaps reward Amelie – even if not without realising – by showing her that keeping things nice meant all would be well – that it equalled safety and security.'

Amanda smiled and nodded. 'I think we're speaking the same language. And I definitely wouldn't worry about the food thing. The issues around eating could just be her reaction to being nervous in a new place with new people. She may have felt anxious, but couldn't find the means to articulate it, and, as I'm sure you know, a lot of young children explain anxiety as an empty feeling in their tummy. They think they can make that go away by eating more. In any event, if you find it steadily improving, then I'd cross it off your list of concerns. Just keep doing what you're doing would seem to be the logical way forward.'

By the time I logged off, though nothing earth-shattering had happened, I felt I at least had a theory that could help me understand our little house guest a bit better. Yes, it *was* just a theory, as we knew so little about Amelie's former life, but it was as good a theory as any, had the benefit of feeling logical, and Amanda had also endorsed what instinct had already taught me I should be doing – that modelling 'normal', in a calm, loving and consistent manner was the best thing I could do, while leaving Amanda herself, since she was the professional in this situation, to delve gently deeper into what made Amelie tick.

What I also had, however, was this keen sense of 'there but by the grace of God go I'. At some point in the past, this sick and now legally incarcerated woman had almost certainly been a mother with the best of intentions towards her undoubtedly beloved child. So however energised I felt after my meeting with Amanda, it was leavened with a big dollop of gratitude and humility, as well as an even greater amount of sympathy for Amelie's mum, and a profound hope that she could find her way back to good mental health. Without a supporting family to help pick up the pieces – something so many of us take too much for granted – what had happened to her could have happened to anyone.

# Chapter 8

I'm not normally one for hexes and jinxes, or worrying about walking under ladders, but when Andy Clarke called, a couple of days after my Teams meeting with the psychologist, I couldn't help thinking I must have had some weird negative influence just by dint of keeping my fingers crossed for positive news.

Andy was calling because he'd had a catch-up email from the hospital who were currently looking after Amelie's mother. 'And I'm afraid,' he said, 'that it isn't good news. I would rather have driven over and delivered it personally, obviously, but with this lockdown palaver we'd have been bellowing across the doorstep, so I thought it best to do it over the phone. Are you okay to talk?'

'Yes, it's fine,' I said, 'Amelie's in the garden with Mike. What's happened?'

'A bit of a head-scratcher to be honest,' he said. 'Apparently Mum's a lot better – back on her meds, largely stable, making some progress – which is why the next bit's so strange. She doesn't want her back, bottom line.'

'What, Amelie?' A silly question. Of course he meant Amelie.

'Yes, apparently she's decided it would be in Amelie's best interests if she permanently relinquishes care of her.'

'What – just like that? With no discussion? And does she mean relinquish care as in forever?'

I couldn't quite get my head around it. Could she really be *compos mentis* enough to make such a big decision? If so, and she truly had Amelie's best interests at heart, then it also represented a monumental, truly horrible sacrifice. As a mother myself, it was hard to take in. 'That feels like a very big decision to make so soon after all this happened,' I said to Andy. 'Is there really that much rush to take such drastic action?'

'I don't think so, at least not from our point of view, but apparently she's adamant. She's already asked the local authority to obtain a care order. They say she's devastated that she put her daughter at such risk,' he went on, 'and seems to understand fully that she's at high risk of going down that road again. She knows she is likely to take herself off meds at any point, as she's done several times in the past, apparently, and that if and when that happens she would be a danger to everyone. To herself and, most importantly, to her little girl.'

'So that's that then?' I asked, still astounded by how quickly Kelly had reached this decision. 'She doesn't even want to try? Take a bit of time? See how things go?'

'She's actually asked for an extended stay at the facility, and it seems she really wants to try to get better this time,' Andy explained, 'but part of her therapy involved her acknowledging how negative an impact her condition has had on Amelie, and she truly believes that the child will be better off without her. I know it feels a bit sudden, a bit brutal, but to be honest with you, I have to say that we, as an authority, have agreed, so we'll be going ahead and making an application for a court order. Which isn't to say we're not actively looking at other options.'

'You mean there are some other options?'

'Well, we can but try. There must be some relatives out there somewhere. And there's obviously a father, of course.'

'Do you know anything about him?'

'Not much. Only that he did a disappearing act when his daughter was just a few months old. He apparently moved to Scotland and started the proverbial new life, so chances are that he may not want anything to do with a long-lost daughter he doesn't even know. But like I say, we'll explore every avenue.'

'So, what do I need to do?' I asked, looking out into the garden and already dreading the conversation I would doubtless now have to have. Even though Amelie had shown very little interest in her mother's well-being or whereabouts, and definitely seemed to have attachment issues, a part of me couldn't help but still be anxiously braced for the whole edifice to come crashing down. Because we might all be wrong, mightn't we? There was still the possibility that Amelie's seeming lack of concern could be an unconscious way of protecting herself. Badly traumatised children often built a carapace around themselves and, the longer that went on, the greater the falling apart when it eventually crumbled and fell.

'Well,' Andy said, 'once we get a court order, as you know, given her age and situation, we'll almost certainly be putting her up for adoption. In the meantime, though, I think the best thing is to let her know that she's definitely going to be staying with you for a good while longer. Then I'll come over in a bit, obviously after the court case, so it will probably be a few weeks yet, to explain to her that she won't be going back to Mum. I know it feels sad,' he finished, 'but it probably *is* in her best interests, don't you think?'

I could only agree, because it probably was. Amelie was young enough to have a chance at a whole new life, free from fear and insecurity, and if Andy *was* right, the alternative future, eventually going back to her mum, would be a highly uncertain one, with the sword of Damocles forever hanging over her.

Still, though, it felt desperately sad, and I really couldn't comprehend the speed at which Mum had made her decision. Which gave me pause for thought. *Was* it sudden, I wondered, or had this been brewing for a while? Perhaps she had decided some time ago that having a child was just too much for her, and this latest episode might just have been the straw that broke the camel's back. And it did sort of figure: Amelie's lack of attachment to her mother didn't exist in a vacuum, after all. Anyway, whatever the reasoning or the background, Amelie had to be told.

After saying goodbye to Andy, I went into the kitchen and finished off the pasta lunch I'd been preparing when he'd called. Then I called Mike and Amelie in, and, while Amelie popped to the loo to wash her hands, quickly filled Mike in on the gist of the conversation.

He wasn't surprised. It was always going to be one of the potential outcomes for the poor girl. Though I think both of us had expected it to be a decision favoured by the authority, given her mum's mental health, rather than coming from the woman herself, and particularly at such an early stage in her recovery.

'I have something important to tell you, sweetheart,' I said to Amelie as the three of us sat down at the dining table and began digging into our food. 'It's about Mummy.'

Amelie continued to wolf down her pasta, and then seemed to realise that I was waiting for some sort of reaction before continuing. 'Oh,' she said, looking across at me, seeming confused. 'You mean *my* mummy? I thought you meant *your* mummy.'

She had seen my mum on FaceTime phone calls a few times lately, so the question was, I supposed, logical. But it seemed telling to me that she'd automatically jump to that confusion.

'Your mummy,' I said. 'You know she's in the hospital, right?'

Amelie nodded, seemingly nonplussed. She loved pasta and, though her odd ways around food were indeed settling down, she still ate at a pace that suggested that she thought that anything put in front of her might be snatched away again at any moment.

'Well, she's still not well enough to look after you, sweetie, and she has asked if you can stay with us for a bit longer. It might actually be for quite a long time, in fact.' I paused at that point to let it sink in and to gauge her reaction, but there was none. 'So for now,' I went on, 'you will live with me and Mike, but it might mean you could end up living with someone else later on. Do you understand, lovely?'

Again, Amelie nodded. Then looked at me and smiled. 'This is nice pasta,' she said enthusiastically. 'Can we have it for tea as well?'

Mike looked at me with raised eyebrows and put his fork down. 'Do you understand what Casey is saying, Amelie?' he asked. 'Because we need to know that you do.'

Amelie put her own fork down and returned Mike's gaze, smiling. 'Of course I do,' she said, suddenly sounding older than her years. 'Mummy is sick, so I can't live with her anymore. My house is burned down and I got no stuff.' She paused, as if considering if she had everything covered. 'Oh, and if this house gets burned down, I have to move in with some other safe guys.'

I could honestly have wept. The smile had never once left her face as she outlined the facts as she saw them. This little girl was effectively homeless now and had none of her physical childhood things. No toys or clothes that were familiar, and probably no photographs or school reports and certificates either. No favourite mug, or special cushion, or seat at a familiar table. All the little things we take for granted. I wondered once again when exactly the impact of all of this was going to finally hit her. Even *if* it was going to hit her. The truth was, I had no idea, and all I could really trust in was the incredible resilience and adaptability of children, and hope that someday soon, being so young, Amelie just might have a stab at a normal, loving life. Hopefully that would mean a new set of adoptive parents, or, against all odds, her birth father stepping up and offering her a lifeline.

Her total lack of concern about not having seen her mother for such a long time worried me even more now. We had spelled out the facts and she'd not so much as asked a question. There was no getting away from it. This would cause huge problems down the line and, no matter how loving and consistent Mike and I resolved to be for the immediate future, there would come a time when Amelie *would* demand answers, and would possibly need a whole new level of professional support if she had any hope of forming those strong human bonds that are taken so much for granted by those of us who have enjoyed them.

It took a good while for me to get my head around the thick red line that had been drawn under Amelie's former life, and I couldn't help but wonder if Amelie's mother had been having similar thoughts. Could she really think that rationally in the aftermath of such a terrific trauma? So when I saw a call come in from Christine a couple of days later, my first thought was that she might have had a change of heart. And it seemed I might be right.

'Kelly has decided she'd like to see Amelie,' she said.

'Really?' I said. 'Well, that's good news, isn't it?' Then I thought about the lockdown. 'But is that even allowed?'

'A video call,' she clarified. 'And, no, I'm not sure it is. I asked if she'd had second thoughts about us obtaining a care order, and apparently she hasn't. She still maintains that she can't – won't – have Amelie back, but until that's all under way officially, she knows that she can still have contact. And she wants it.'

'But why?'

'She hasn't enlightened us. She just knows her rights and apparently wishes to exercise them.'

'But isn't that only going to confuse things for Amelie? And given that, don't you have the power to ask more first? Surely "best interests" can be factored in here?'

'Partly. So it's been made clear to her that Amelie doesn't really understand what it all means, in terms of her relinquishing care to us, and that she can't discuss any of that with her – those are our terms – at least not until Andy has been out for his chat. So she has agreed to keep things simple, and to not talk about what's going to happen in the future. But she *does* want the video call, and, as she says, she's allowed that. So assuming you're okay with that, we'd like to set it up for tomorrow. We'll get a nurse to supervise things from the hospital.'

So what was this, I wondered? Was it guilt? Despite what Christine said, could it possibly be indicative of a change of heart? A part of me wondered if it was a way for her to check if she'd made the right decision. Testing her resolve, perhaps, that to relinquish Amelie was indeed the best way forward. So I agreed, of course. Obviously for Amelie's sake primarily, but also to satisfy my own curiosity. And I *was* curious. So I hoped I'd get a glimpse into what made Kelly tick. Knowledge was power, after all.

'Oh, and as I say, Casey, if she *does* go down any avenues that you feel uncomfortable with, given what I've just said, you are within *your* rights to end the call.'

Great. So Amelie might not have a care in the world, but now I did.

# Chapter 9

I had decided the day before that I wouldn't prepare Amelie for the phone call with her mum. 'She might not sleep if I do,' I'd said to Mike, 'either with worry, or excitement. She just seems like one of those kids who do better in the here and now, so I'm going to leave it until breakfast before telling her about the call. That way we'll only have an hour or so to deal with whatever feelings the news provokes.'

'Which could be interesting,' he'd said. 'This could be a bit of a clincher, couldn't it? Actually seeing her mum might be a game-changer, bless her. Might be the point at which the reality finally hits her.' He glanced across at where Amelie was curled up in her pyjamas, curls still damp from her recent bath, and her tablet on her lap, cartoons chuntering away quietly, as per usual, while we cleared up tea before I read her a bedtime story. 'Either way,' he said, 'we're going to learn something useful.'

He was right about that, but what should we be hoping for, I wondered? For Amelie to see her mum and continue on as if she really wasn't that bothered about being apart from her, or the kind of total meltdown that would very much prove she was? Despite the distress that would cause her, not least now we knew Mum was relinquishing care of her, I couldn't help hoping that was going to happen, since an emotionless child was always far more of challenge, both to care for, and for adoptive parents to genuinely bond with and grow to love. There were amazing people out there that relished taking on the sort of children they would get very little back from emotionally (and thank goodness for them), but lots, not unreasonably, wanted to adopt children they could bring up and cherish as their own. Forget Amelie not sleeping – I really struggled that night. I was really beginning to miss my own children and grandchildren. FaceTime really didn't cut it. And the contrast between that and the bleak FaceTime I would be overseeing, come the morning, made me feel uncharacteristically down and sad.

Still, as Mike had said, this would be a great learning opportunity, which could only help us in our continuing care of Amelie, and by the time we were sitting down for boiled eggs and soldiers the following morning, I was up for the challenge, and in the right frame of mind.

'Oh, I almost forgot, Amelie,' I said, smiling at her as I took my seat at the table, 'your mummy is going to FaceTime you this morning. Won't that be nice?'

Mike and I were both scanning her face to get some sense of her reaction, but there was none. 'On my iPad,' she asked casually, 'or on your phone?'

'Um, actually, my laptop,' I said. 'My phone is linked up to it, so I'll set it all up at the table, then you and Mummy can settle down for a nice chat. How do you feel about that?' I added as she stuck her spoon in her decapitated egg. 'Talking with Mummy, I mean.'

Amelie paused with her spoon in mid-air, as if giving the question serious consideration. She then smiled a big smile, which didn't seem exactly forced, but definitely *did* seem performative. She was smiling, I thought, because she knew a smile was expected. The thought was backed up straight afterwards, too. 'I'm so excited! I miss Mummy, don't I?'

*Don't I?* Such an odd way of putting things. Had someone said that to her often? *You miss Mummy, don't you?* I glanced at Mike before answering. 'I imagine you do, sweetie, so it'll be really nice to have a catch-up with her, won't it? And you can tell her all about your new room, and all the lovely pictures you've painted, oh, and about how you might be going to a new school for a while. You'll certainly have lots to talk about, won't you?'

Amelie nodded, and smiled again, before biting into a piece of toast. Then swallowed and frowned. 'But I can't do it on your laptop. If I talk to Mummy on your laptop, she won't know it's safe. She'll think there's bugs or FBI mens, and she'll get cross. I think we need to do it on my tablet. For security.'

I almost changed my mind then, but instinct told me to do no such thing. This was a child of six! And she was talking as though we were about to be holding a high-level secret international summit. Surely I shouldn't be playing into the woman's fantasies?

'I'm sure she won't be cross at all,' I said instead. 'She will be that happy to see you on the screen that she won't even be *thinking* about things like that, I'm sure of it. And we both know all the computers and phones here are safe, so we can both reassure her, can't we?'

This seemed to reassure Amelie sufficiently that she was back tucking into her egg again – indeed, only seconds later she was asking Mike what the next job in the garden was going to be and how long it was going to be till they could set up the hot tub, which had arrived the previous day. Security issues aside, she really was that nonplussed by it all.

For my own part, I could only hope I was right. It had been hard to build up a picture of Amelie's mum that didn't get coloured by her various conspiracy theories, but she was back on her medication so presumably the picture in my head no longer applied, and all that kind of stuff was in the past. I mentally crossed my fingers, because, with all that lay ahead, this phone call needed to be positive, for Amelie's sake.

Breakfast finished, I cleared the dining table and set up my laptop, and ten minutes before the call time, and with everything in place, a change came over Amelie.

She started talking to me in her baby babble, and for the first time in a good couple of weeks.

'Me need wibbons,' she said, pouting, 'my mamma wuvs me with wibbons in my hair. Me wanna look pwetty. Can you make me look pretty? So Mumma wuvs me?'

'Your hair is just fine as it is, lovely,' I said firmly. 'And please talk like a big girl, Amelie. You're six, remember? Not a baby. I need you speak properly, please, when Mummy calls, okay?'

There was another pout, and then a small rebuke. 'You should have curled my hair last night, if you knew about the FaceTime. And put some ribbons in. Mummy will be sad now and she might even *cry*. And it's not my fault.'

I honestly thought that Amelie was about to cry herself then, which was the last thing I wanted, but just at that moment my phone and laptop both started ringing, signalling that I was being video-called. I glanced at Amelie, but the sad face had now been replaced by a beaming smile, and she jumped onto the chair that I'd set out for her.

'Mamma!' she said, as the screen came to life, and now her excitement seemed genuine. 'Mamma! I love you! Have you missed me?'

Though I didn't yet know if this would be a one-off event or a series of virtual encounters, protocol demanded that I stay next to Amelie for the duration of the call so I pulled up my own chair and smiled at the woman whose face now filled the screen. I don't know quite what I had expected, but I'd obviously formed some kind of mental image because the first thing I thought was: *Is this really her? Have I been put through to the wrong person entirely?* Because the woman staring back at me – and yes, she was really staring, more at me than at her daughter – was beautiful, in that stop and do a double-take kind of way, and had a composure about her that seemed completely at odds with the shrieking woman who threw computers up into the air. Which just goes to show how one should try not to form views based on third-hand information. It was also a reminder why mental illness could be so stigmatising and how vivid negative images of it can be.

As I took her in, Kelly continued to regard me, unabashedly and coolly, while not yet responding in any way to Amelie. She looked to be in her mid-thirties and the sleek blonde glossy hair that fell almost to her waist was either a gift from the hair gods or had been straightened. I favoured the latter, concocting another, different, picture; that of a healthcare assistant at the hospital going above and beyond to make sure the patient looked her very best. Even brighter than Amelie's, Kelly's eyes were a vivid icy blue, framed by long lashes and beautifully applied make-up. So she clearly had access to beauty products in the facility, and perhaps somebody had bought her new clothes as well, I thought, because she looked very smart in a grey floral blouse – all I could see of her, but obviously a whole world away from the smoky-smelling clothes her daughter had arrived at our house in those scant few weeks earlier.

Only seconds had passed, but Kelly's constant gaze on me was oddly intimidating, not least due to her continuing silence. Was there some kind of satellite delay perhaps?

'Hi,' I said, smiling at both her and the nurse that was standing, half off-screen, to her left. 'I'm Casey. Nice to meet you at last, even if only virtually.'

'If that's a dig at me,' she responded immediately, 'don't think I won't be making a note of it.'

*Woah*. That definitely stopped me in my tracks. 'Not at all,' I began, shocked. 'I just meant …'

She raised a hand to silence me. 'Forget it,' she said. 'And I'm here to speak to my daughter, not you, so if you could just, you know, go off and get on with something, please.'

I couldn't remember the last time I'd gone from calm and relaxed to seething anger in such a short space of time. No, correction. I couldn't remember it happening ever. Annoyingly, my cheeks were also now burning from embarrassment, when I had absolutely nothing to be embarrassed about. Happily, I was saved from having to come up with an answer, because the nurse immediately leaned further into the frame and pointed out that just as she had to supervise the call from their end, so did I at my end, so I'd be staying.

'Well, that's just *great*,' Kelly snapped, scowling at her, her anger now redirected, but I could see from the nurse's benign, but 'you know the rules' expression that it was only for effect. Within a heartbeat she had changed her expression completely. 'Hello darling!!' she exclaimed, beaming delightedly, almost as if she'd only just noticed her daughter was sitting beside me. 'It's so good to see your beautiful little face. How are you doing? Are they treating you well?'

Well, I've learned one thing, I thought, as I watched their curious conversational dance begin. It wasn't only Amelie who could turn the beam on and off at will. I was also fascinated to see Amelie immediately return to the baby babble, which didn't seem to faze her mother in the least. Well, either she understood it and expected it, or simply chose to go along with it – either way, it was a pretty odd way of communicating; more like a grandmother cooing over the pram of a tiny gurgling baby than two people with actual words at their disposal. Or, I thought, straight after that, like someone would address a small dog.

I was glad now, in fact, about how studiously Kelly ignored me. While I might have expected there to be at least some element of communication – a question, an affirmation of something Amelie was saying to her, *something* – she acted as if I was invisible, which left me free to take in, and take note of, anything I could which might aid my understanding of their relationship. But then she crossed a line, when discussing Amelie's food, because she started talking *about* me. And, even more galling, doing it as if I wasn't there.

'Oh, my very favowite,' Amelie babbled at her, 'is pasta, with ham and cheese. And with special red sauce. It's yummy yum delicious. Mummy, you should try it!'

Amelie turned to me then, as if about to ask me to share the recipe, but my burgeoning polite smile was quickly wiped off my face.

'Fucking pasta?' Kelly snapped, glaring at the nurse. 'On the money they get fucking fostering? They're taking the fucking piss!'

Now she addressed me directly. 'You feed my child shit like that? That's it, I'm reporting you. My daughter needs a freshly cooked meal every day.' She raised the hand again, this time displaying manicured fingers, with which she listed my transgressions one by one. 'She needs meat. Fish and chicken. She needs nuts, and fruit and vegetables. She needs the *smallest* amount of carbohydrate –' she pinched finger and thumb together to illustrate – 'and she doesn't need fucking ketchup slapped all over everything!'

I watched the nurse's hand slowly snake out and then land, without accompanying comment or fanfare, on Kelly's nearest forearm. To which Kelly responded, '*What?* I'm not having this! I mean it! They take fucking liberties, the lot of them' – she stabbed a finger at me – 'and she's no different!'

'Kelly,' the nurse said calmly, 'calm down, okay?'

She might well have said the same to me. While Amelie continued to sit there with the same fixed smile she'd had on her face since the call had started – an oddness that wasn't lost on me – I was properly fuming. I knew there was no point in my arguing back, or pointing out that we had made fresh tomato sauces together, or that, in fact, pasta, cheese, ham and tomatoes was a balanced meal, and in any case just one of many different, equally healthy ones we cooked. No point in doing anything, in fact, other than smile back, just like Amelie, and bite my tongue.

The cheek of it wasn't lost on me, however. This woman was acting like I'd stolen her daughter from her. Not that she'd almost burnt the house down and had Amelie removed for her own safety, not that her illness had prevented her from actually being a mother herself. No, it seemed that this situation was all my fault. I made a mental note that if there was any reporting to be done, it would be me doing it. This was all wrong. I shouldn't have to sit here and be abused in my own home, either in person or over a screen. I decided then and there that I would be telling Christine that unless Kelly changed her attitude towards me then I certainly wouldn't be supervising any more calls. A social worker would have to come out and do it because this would be the last time I took this kind of rudeness, especially in front of Amelie. It was no wonder some children hated the system; if they witnessed this kind of warring, rather than a united front, from all the adults who were supposed to have their best interests at heart, I wasn't at all surprised.

By now, Kelly had told her accompanying nurse she could go and 'do one as well', and Amelie seemed to rouse herself finally from her smiling torpor. 'There's no FBI mens here, Mamma,' she said, now back using her proper voice, 'and no bugs, none at all. And I have a beautiful bedroom, with lots of books and toys and dollies. It's safe here, I'm okay, it's *very safe* here.'

Giving no indication that she had ever thought otherwise (well, apart from the diet from hell we were apparently feeding her), Kelly glared at me before turning on a smile again for her daughter. 'Now you know, sweet cheeks,' she said, 'that that was all just a silly game Mummy played. We know it's not *real* though, sweet cheeks, don't we?'

Amelie's expression was now one of surprise and confusion. Then something seemed to click in her brain and she nodded – a nod that was somewhat over-egged. 'I *know*. Just a silly game, that's what we always say.' She leaned towards the screen. 'Mamma,' she said, glancing at me then cupping a hand around her mouth, 'is it okay,' she whispered, 'for Casey *to know*?'

Kelly blinked once, then stood up and turned to the nurse. 'I need to go back to my room, please,' she snapped. Then she turned back to Amelie. 'I have to go now, darling. I need my medicine. You be a good girl, okay? Mummy loves you.'

*What?* I thought. Barely 20 minutes had passed. Was that it? Clearly yes, as Kelly was moving away from the screen now, blowing Amelie kisses as she backed out of the room. Beneath the gauzy blouse, I noticed, were a pair of scruffy off-black trackie bottoms, not unlike several pairs I also owned. The words 'smoke and mirrors' seemed poignantly apt.

The nurse spoke only briefly, to say goodbye and to thank us for our time. Then, just before the call disconnected and the screen went black, I found myself staring at a still of a completely empty room. Had that even just happened?

I turned to Amelie, reached out and gave her a hug. 'Well, that was lovely, wasn't it?' I said, smelling her shampoo-fresh hair. 'Being able to see Mummy?'

But she was already wriggling out of my grasp. She'd seen Mike over my shoulder. I turned to see him doing a thumbs-up. 'Hot tubbbbbb!!' Amelie whooped. 'It's time to fill the hot tub!'

I let her go, marvelling that the communication between her and Mike – all those thumbs-up and high fives and fist bumps – were a good deal more edifying and uncomplicated to witness than the weirdness that had been the last half hour or so. I would let them get on with it for a bit, I thought, and write everything up while they were otherwise engaged. I didn't want to damn and be judgemental, nor did I want to cause trouble, but I still felt very aggrieved to have been spoken to the way I had, and I wanted that out of my system. We didn't do what we did for gratitude – particularly from birth parents, some of whom might always see us as the enemy, or not have the capacity to even know what we did. No, we did it to help. Because it fulfilled us to make a difference. Right now, and I was willing to have my impressions corrected, obviously, the biggest difference would be made to Amelie's life if she did as her mother apparently wished; say farewell to her, to that whole life, and to move on to a brighter future.

I brought up the log on my laptop just as Amelie returned, now decked out in her new favourite cossie and carrying the big Little Mermaid beach towel – one of Marley Mae's old favourites – that she loved.

'Are you coming in?' she asked. 'Come *on*. We're celebrating! You *have* to!'

And her face was such a picture, so full of 'in-the-moment' excitement, that there really wasn't any other answer than, 'Yes, lovely, of course I am. I'll get changed and then I'll be there, tout suite!'

I was just following her out, my own cossie now donned, when something else occurred to me.

Perhaps Amelie had worked that out as well.

# Chapter 10

I kept a close eye on Amelie over the next few days, just to check that the screen contact with her mother hadn't had any negative impact on her. It certainly didn't appear to have. In fact, the opposite seemed to be true. She seemed her usual sunny self and the only unsolicited mention she made of her mother's name had been the day after the FaceTime, when we were out in the garden painting.

Her picture was mostly grass and daisies, but at the far edge there was a very tiny building – a house that barely reached the top of the stems of grass. I thought of the film *Signs* again, of the stricken family home being surrounded by towering corn fields. Were the images Amelie created all from imagination, or had some of them been imprinted on her brain?

'What's that?' I asked her, pointing to the tiny dwelling. 'Is it somewhere you know?'

She shook her head. 'No. It's Mummy's safe house in the butterfly meadow. 'Cept there aren't any butterflies yet because they don't come till summer.'

'I think I'd love to live in the middle of a butterfly meadow,' I told her. 'I think Mummy would like it there too, don't you?'

'You think my mummy *is* safe in her safe house?' she asked, after a period of silence. 'Do you think any monsters might find her there?'

I put my own paintbrush down so she could see she had my full attention, and answered her seriously and slowly. 'Mummy is very safe there, Amelie, and is being well cared for. For the time being, her safe house is a hospital, so there are doctors, and nurses, and all sorts of other kind people, and I'm sure she'll have made some friends there too. And I am absolutely sure there are no monsters there at all.'

Amelie nodded, as if satisfied. 'Yeah, I think so too,' she said, immediately going back to her painting. 'My picture is almost done now. Have you finished yours yet?'

I looked down at my masterpiece. An artist, I was not. Some might look at my 'work' and assume I was a Lowry fan, but the truth was that flat, square buildings and matchstick men were the absolute limit of my abilities. It didn't matter. There was something rather special about having all this unallocated time with our little foster child. Thanks to the pandemic, there were no competing demands. No errands to run. No work rotas for Mike to be mindful of. No necessity to run anything to an outside or self-imposed schedule. And though I knew some sessions at school would be welcome and good for Amelie, this too – this gift of time to play with her – was really very pleasant. It was also, little by little, opening the window up on her world. And there was a thought: perhaps we could plant up a butterfly meadow. Or at least fill a pot with some butterfly-friendly plants.

'Pretty much,' I said, surveying my floral effort and wishing I'd opted for my usual beach scene with brightly coloured fishes (essentially, just a few sideways number 8s with tails). 'We'll call Mike over to judge who is the winner, shall we?'

Mike, who was busy sawing wood in the back of the shed, was more than happy to come across and pronounce Amelie's the winner. Needless to say, he was never nervous about judging an art competition between me and a child. 'I absolutely always know which one is yours, Casey,' he once said when I asked him how he could always tell. 'I've never met anyone, adult or child, who paints or draws quite as badly!' Safe to say, the child always got the number-one spot!

'By the way,' he said, 'I've just been catching up with the Covid news on the radio. Looks like we can actually go out as much as we like now, *and* meet up with one other person as well – well, as long as it's outside, in public, and socially distanced, and in a public place. So that's something, isn't it?'

This was indeed fabulous news. It meant I could actually see the kids and grandkids at last and though I wasn't allowed to hug them yet, it felt thrilling to know we'd be able to see one another in person at last. I had never in my life been physically separated from all my children and grandchildren for so long. And though I was desperate for us all to have a big family gathering, just the thought that I'd be able to amble round the park with Riley filled me with joy. It seemed, at long last, that we were getting there.

It also looked like we were back in demand for a bit of respite because that same evening, Christine phoned to ask if we'd accept another 48-hour placement.

'I don't know if you know the McKays,' she said. 'They live just out of the area, but I'm sure you'll have come across Sheila at one of the training days.'

I tried to place the name but couldn't. 'I'm not sure,' I said. 'Why? Does one of her children need to come to us to give her a break?'

'Not one. Two,' Christine said. 'She's actually one of our dedicated mother and baby foster carers. Trouble is, she's had one teenage girl and her baby boy there for six months, and they're really settled, but just before lockdown, we asked her to take on another young mum and her two-month-old baby girl. It was only meant to be for a short assessment after which she was to be placed elsewhere, but of course the whole world changed and she had to stay put. We literally have nowhere else to send them at the moment.'

'Right,' I said, still unsure about what I was being asked to do. 'And it's all a bit too much for Shelia, I'm guessing.'

'You could say that. The truth is that the two teenage girls really do not get along. I mean, *really* do not get along. And with the new one a year or so older, she tends to intimidate the first girl. You'd think they'd have enough to do caring for a baby apiece, wouldn't you? But they still seem to find time to fall out … It's like World War Three at Sheila's most days. It's been getting to the stage where the long-term girl hardly comes out of her room anymore, bless her, just to stay out of the new girl's way.'

'A bit of a handful then, is she?'

'More than a bit, it seems. Quite a headstrong girl, apparently, and difficult to manage; I don't know a great deal about her, but she apparently has quite a few issues. Seems to be the sort of girl who'd pick a fight in an empty room. Sheila just wants a couple of days' break from it all so she can spend a bit of quality time with her long-term mum and baby – and perhaps bring about a bit of a reset in the dynamic. I know it's looking like we'll be able to move the girl on next month, fingers crossed, once they ease a few more restrictions, but, in the meantime, I think a couple of days' respite will make the next couple of weeks a little easier for Sheila to cope with. She's also afraid if this tension gets any worse, it might jeopardise the original placement, and the girl was doing so well before Katie turned up. That's the girl we want you to have, by the way – she and her baby daughter, Jasmine.

'And, of course,' Christine continued, 'if anyone can manage a challenging teen, you and Mike can. As long as all's well with little Amelie, that is? Sounds as if you didn't have the most edifying experience with Mum the other day, but she's still bobbing along relatively unperturbed?'

I looked across to the living area, where Amelie was on the sofa with Mike, who was reading her a bedtime story. 'Completely,' I confirmed. 'And I know she'll be thrilled to have another baby in the house to fuss over. So yes, of course. More than happy to help.'

And I was. It sounded like something Mike and I could easily handle, especially for a mere 48 hours, and Christine was right; it really did sound like a time-out was needed for the two warring teenagers. A break from each other might be just what was needed to find a way through the discord. I also knew how important it might be to them. It must have been awful for Sheila and her husband, living through all that, and especially while trying to assess the young mothers' suitability to be able to raise their own children. Fights and arguments did not look good on reports being sent to the courts.

'This weekend then?' Christine asked. 'Give you a day to get organised for them? Oh, and there is one thing I – ahem – need to mention. Although Katie is 18 and can technically leave the home whenever she wants, she can't take the baby with her, under any circumstances.'

Alarm bells started ringing then. Was Katie a danger to her baby? And would I be putting Amelie at risk, having her with us? 'You're going to have to tell me why, Chris,' I said, 'because if she's going to be any risk to Amelie, I'd obviously have to change my mind.'

'No, it's not that,' she reassured me. 'Good heavens, woman. What do you take me for?' She chuckled then. 'Wily, yes. You know me. But I wouldn't have asked you if that were the case. She poses absolutely no risk to Amelie. More to herself, truth be known. Plus, she knows the laws and how they can serve her purpose. You'd think an 18-year-old young mother would relish the chance to go out alone and leave her baby to be looked after by her foster carer, but not Katie.'

'Oh right,' I said, bemused. 'Is it that she's over-protective or something?'

Christine laughed. 'Not a bit,' she said. 'In fact, it seems baby Jasmine is something of a useful accessory. Yes, she helps give the impression that Katie is a loving, attentive mother – and I have to say that there have been no real red flags as concerns her day-to-day care of her daughter, according to Sheila – but the reality is that it's more about her need for a pram and blankets. Katie is a bit of a problem drinker and the minute she's out of the house she's usually headed for the nearest off-licence. If she has no money, she steals it. Vodka usually, Sheila tells me, the pram and blankets being the perfect hiding place for any contraband she manages to get hold of. Poor Jasmine – just two months old – is already an innocent mule, to all intents and purposes.'

It was a pretty harsh way of putting it, but I knew where Christine was coming from. Having lost her own baby to cot death a couple of decades previously, she couldn't help but feel personally aggrieved when she came upon situations like this one. She was always scrupulously professional, of course, but I still picked up on the slight edge to her voice when dealing with young mums who neglected or mistreated their own babies in any way. And I totally understood where she was coming from.

And Amelie was, of course, full of excitement. She was a little disappointed when I explained that at two months old, little Jasmine wouldn't be quite old enough to play schools with her, but she soon switched tack and decided that since Jasmine would be just like a little dolly, she would be able to help her mother with bathing her and putting ribbons in her hair and dressing and undressing her in all the baby clothes I had in my baby-clothes box in the spare room.

'Well, maybe not *too* much of that,' I was at pains to impress upon her. 'Tiny babies mostly just want to sleep and have their feeds,' I explained, 'but I'm sure her mummy will be only too glad to have someone to help them with all the nappy changes. And she might even let you push her pram around the garden with her if the weather stays nice.'

That seemed to be sufficient of a revised agenda for Amelie and she went up to bed both happy and full of plans for the weekend, and keen to spend the following day doing a selection of paintings for them both, and arranging 'welcome teddies' in the bedroom I was going to put them in.

In fact, the only sad note was when I tucked her into bed and she suddenly sighed, a pained expression on her face.

'I just had a thought,' she said. 'The twins' teddies.'

'The twins' teddies?' I asked, instantly alert to the emotional change. This was the first mention she'd made of twins since Layla and Harlan had stayed.

She looked at me with big, anxious eyes. 'They were in our burned-down house. Do you think they've gone to the same heaven?'

I wanted to marshal my thoughts before answering. 'The same heaven?' I asked, to buy myself a couple of moments.

'The same heaven as the twins live,' she explained. 'Animals go over the rainbow bridge when they die. Now the teddies have died too, will they have gone to the right place? Is the rainbow bridge heaven the same heaven as the people one?'

It was a question I'd never heard before, let alone thought about. I knew people posted on social media about beloved pets going 'over the rainbow bridge' when they passed away, but had never thought about a child perhaps feeling anxious about soft toys being reunited with deceased owners.

Amelie clearly had though. 'Mummy kept them in a special box. I don't think she remembered that they'd die too.' She trailed off, the question clearly making her feel upset.

'Well, funnily enough,' I said firmly, 'I know for a *fact* that there is a special place in heaven where lost toys are sent, *specially* so they can be sent on to any children who are up in heaven and might have lost them. It's a whole department which is in charge of doing just that. So, yes, absolutely, they will be together again, so you have no need to worry.'

The anxiety melted away from her immediately. 'That's good,' she said. And that was pretty much all she said. Another quick story and she was asleep in a matter of moments.

For me, though, the picture couldn't help but linger, and the woman who'd so enraged me on FaceTime melted away to be replaced by a very different one; now the picture was of a young mother who'd clearly suffered a terrible, terrible tragedy. *Had* that been the root of her illness? It was easy for Mike to judge my terrible artwork. Rather harder for me to stand in judgement over Amelie's mother. I resolved I'd try very hard, going forward, not to do so.

# Chapter 11

Friday afternoon saw Mike and I – with Amelie, of course, jumping up and down excitedly in front of us – masked up in our doorway and wondering who was about to step out of the car that had pulled up outside our house. Rather than the foster carer herself doing the transportation, this time it was someone from the local authority, who I didn't doubt was relishing the opportunity to be out and about on a sunny Friday afternoon.

'The McKays are a bit tied up,' the woman called across, from where she was dealing with a baby carrier on the back seat. 'I'm Sarah Townend,' she added, 'Katie's social worker. Don't worry about coming out, I'll bring baby and everything to you.'

I gave her a thumbs-up, feeling that now-familiar sense of impotence and frustration that all the usual interactions were currently so skewed. I was happy to go and help but you couldn't just assume people were happy *for* you to do so. Some were rigorous in keeping away from everyone because they were really very scared, after all. Or, conversely, thought *you* might be. It was a minefield. There was probably all sorts of stuff to be unloaded, as well, not least the baby and the already infamous buggy. And, of course, the mum herself, Katie, who was clambering out of the front passenger seat now, having spent a few moments staying put and furiously texting. And, I noted, was not exactly rushing to help. I wondered how she felt about having been temporarily banished from her carer's house. Annoyed? Or maybe sensing new opportunities? My hunch was briefly the former, and very soon after that the latter. She might have felt miffed that she'd been shipped off with little warning, but Christine's rough sketch made me think she was probably the sort of girl who wouldn't waste much time turning this situation to her advantage if she could.

Perhaps not quite yet though. She definitely looked irritable as she emerged from the car, the high ponytail she'd fashioned from her long, dark brown hair swishing about as she surveyed her new surroundings, and in brushing a speck of something from the leg of her sporty designer tracksuit. She had on the whitest, cleanest pair of trainers I'd seen in a long time.

'I don't think she likes us,' Amelie whispered as she clutched my hand. 'She isn't smiling.'

'She's just nervous,' I answered quietly. 'Some people can't help looking cross when they're nervous. And she doesn't know us yet, does she? She'll soon find out how nice we are.'

The pile of belongings disgorged from the boot, and with Katie having begrudgingly taken ownership of the baby carrier, the trio – social worker, mum and teeny tiny baby Jasmine – were soon standing at what I assume Sarah Townend had estimated was the regulation social distancing spot on our front path. (I wondered if half the planet had by now learned to estimate exactly what distance was 2 metres …) 'Over to you, then!' she said brightly. 'And I'll be back to pick you up again at roughly this time Sunday, Katie. Remember everything we discussed on the way, okay?'

'Okay, *whevs* …' Katie responded, though with a smile in her voice. I imagined the relationship between the girl and her long-suffering social worker was, from their exchange, not without warmth.

It was a different matter once Sarah had left and we'd brought everything inside, however, where a slightly tense awkward atmosphere prevailed. I could see Katie assessing everything, her eyes darting around, taking it all in, her former self-possession gone away. As well it might. She was, after all, an 18-year-old, suddenly deposited among strangers.

'I know this must all be very strange, Katie,' I said, 'to be brought to ours at short notice like this, but honestly, we're very laid-back here, and you can treat our home as if it were yours, okay?'

'Follow me,' Mike said cheerfully, as if to illustrate.

'Me and Amelie will show you where your room is so you can get settled in – Casey is more than happy to watch the baby.'

Katie glanced at her daughter, who was sleeping peacefully in the car seat. Then she shrugged. 'Okay,' she said, 'though there's not much point in me unpacking. I'm only going to be here for, like, a *day*.'

'Well, at least we can take your stuff up,' Mike suggested. 'And Amelie can't wait to show you all the things she's done to make your stay with us feel special, can you, Amelie?'

Amelie, shy now, and, I thought, slightly frightened of Katie, looked longingly towards me and the baby, her eyes telling me she would rather stay with us. But her pride in her welcome paintings, her homemade bunting and array of carefully selected soft toys got the better of her. Placing a hand in Mike's, she led the way back out into the hallway.

Alone with the baby, I knelt down and took her in. It was early days, of course, and she was obviously sleeping, but I could see she was a beautiful little poppet, with long-lashed eyes and delicate features. Which could only lead me to a second thought – what did the future hold for her? The scant notes I'd received from Katie's foster carer the previous day had told me that drugs and alcohol had been a major issue, as had Katie's choice of boyfriends. 'She goes for the "bad boys"', the notes had said, and had refused to give up the current boyfriend in order to be allowed to take her daughter home from hospital. It appeared the mother and baby unit placement had been offered to give Katie the chance to turn her life around, otherwise she would lose Jasmine, and the authorities would take over her care. She now had very little time left to persuade them otherwise.

It was a sad scenario, and more common than anyone would probably imagine: more and more newborns were entering the care system in this way. Still, there was no point in my dwelling too much on this case. It wasn't mine to meddle in, or give too much head-space to, either, and I was just happy that there were plenty of foster carers able to take in and look after little babies like Jasmine until loving adoptive parents were found. Of course, the hope was that with the right nurturing, most of these young mothers would learn how to prioritise their babies, and fight like hell to keep them. Would Katie take up that fight? I could only hope so.

And the first signs were positive. After the slightly awkward beginning, the tension soon eased, and the next couple of hours went well. Katie came down for some tea, and then allowed Amelie to help her feed and dress Jasmine, and even offered to do some drawing with her, up in her and Jasmine's room, while the baby slept downstairs with us, which thrilled Amelie no end.

'Oh gosh! Thank you *so* much,' she gushed. 'Shall I go and get my art box? You can share all my colours with me!'

Mike and I grinned at each other as the pair headed off upstairs. 'You never know,' he said, 'this could just be a walk in the park,' he said. 'And even better, she's keeping Amelie entertained for us, which means I can crack on with some proper work in peace for a change.'

I knew he was half-joking, but that there was a grain of truth: he'd done more than his fair share of entertaining Amelie. Not to mention me. And I knew he must be missing some alone time. He'd probably enjoy a bit of time on his own in the shed.

I laughed. 'Go on then,' I said. 'But *please* do start counting chickens while you're down there.'

I should have heeded my own advice. An hour after going upstairs, Katie was suddenly behind me in the kitchen, and busy tucking Jasmine into her buggy. She'd obviously come down and taken her out of the car seat before I'd even realised she was there.

'Oh, are you putting her down there for a nap?' I asked as I dried my hands on the tea towel. I looked behind her for Amelie, but she was nowhere to be seen. I turned back to Katie: 'Has Amelie been okay?'

'She's fine,' she said. 'She's putting all her crayons and stuff away. I'm just off out for a walk now, with little one, for our one hour of exercise. Well, they say an hour, don't they, but now and again it does take a bit longer, doesn't it? I mean, the government can't judge how long the queues in the shops will be, can they?'

So she obviously wasn't up to speed with the easing of restrictions, but I wasn't about to be the one to tell her. I was in a bind. She'd been with us only a couple of hours, and already we were in a conflict situation. *Under no circumstances* was I supposed to let her go out with the baby on her own and here she was planning on doing exactly that. It was clearly time for my mettle to be tested. Did she expect trouble or for me to be a pushover? So, how to play it? I really didn't want to be in the middle of a massive argument so soon into the weekend.

'Tell you what,' I said lightly, slipping the folded tea towel over the oven door handle, 'I'll ask Mike to watch Amelie for a bit and I'll come with you. I could do with a walk.'

A glare appeared instantly on her previously friendly face. 'No, you can't,' she said, shaking her head. 'I need some time by myself. Me and Jasmine do. It's for my mental health,' she added lamely.

I sighed. We both knew we were playing a game here. 'Look, Katie,' I said, matching her stony glare with one of this-is-how-it-is-then resignation. 'I know you know the rules, just like I do. You can't go out with the baby by yourself. Not yet, at least. You *know* that.'

The stony glare was upped a notch, to anger. 'You're not my proper foster carer,' she said icily. 'And you've no right interfering. I can do what I like.'

'No, Katie. I'm afraid you can't,' I said firmly. 'Now, I'll be two minutes sorting things here with Mike, then, if you want to take Jasmine for a walk, I will be coming *with* you.'

'That's ridiculous!' she huffed, in the tone of a petulant 10-year-old. Then raised her voice further. 'That is fucking *ridiculous*.' I was aware of Amelie walking into the room at that very moment. Which made me cross too.

'Nevertheless,' I said calmly, 'that's what has to happen.'

'No it isn't.' She was shouting now. 'You can't tell me what to do! I'm 18. An adult. *Remember*?'

Thankfully, Mike came in from the garden then, perhaps having heard the commotion, and scooped a visibly upset Amelie up. 'Come on, kiddo,' he said, smiling at her, ignoring Katie completely. 'Time for me and you to go for a bike ride. What do you say?'

With Mike and Amelie out of the way, I decided to try again with Katie, who, as the baby had started crying now, was furiously rocking the pram back and forth.

'Please keep a civil tongue in your head, Katie. You're upsetting your baby and you're also upsetting Amelie. She's not used to shouting and swearing, and, to be honest, neither are we. You know very well that it's part of your placement rules that you're not left unsupervised with Jasmine when you leave the house, so if you're going out with her, I'm coming too and that's that.' To make the point further, I went and fetched my handbag and door keys. 'So,' I said, 'are we going out or not?'

I sensed a deflation then, a battle she'd thought winnable having been lost. 'Oh, you lot are all the same,' she said, her voice still raised, but with a defeatist whining quality I sensed was part of day-to-day life at Sheila's. 'Rules. Fucking rules all the time. I'm alright left unsupervised to do all the night feeds, and to listen to her crying all night, aren't I? No one wants to jump in and do that shit, do they? *Fine!* But if you're coming with me then you need to show me where the nearest supermarket is cos I need more baby milk and stuff. I got my Universal Credit today, so ...' And then she huffed off down the hall, all attitude and strop.

I took the win. All the bluster was water off a duck's back to me. I'd heard it all before, of course. I could write a book on all the shouting and swear words I'd heard. The important thing was that the lines had been drawn. And it was perfectly pleasant to do the 15-minute or so walk to the local supermarket, and be out in the fresh air. Yes, the garden was coming along beautifully – it had never been so closely tended – but there was nothing like getting out and about after so many long weeks of being told to stay at home. Mad what we took for granted, really. Katie, however, didn't seem too thrilled to be walking with an escort and made it clear that she wanted to remain a few yards behind me. I didn't let it spoil my mood.

What I didn't know though, and perhaps Katie did, was that seemingly the rules had changed overnight regarding shopping *en masse*. I was used to seeing queues these days outside all shops that were open, and people in masks standing on newly painted white lines, set 3 feet apart. Now, however, instead of a whole family being allowed in together, it seemed to have changed. I had no idea what was happening in other shops – Mike and I had commented more than once that everyone seemed to be interpreting the rules differently – but, as we stood in the queue, watching person after person having stuff explained to them and then family members being turned away, the new rule was fast becoming clear: only one person from each family was allowed inside the shop, the only exception being single mothers with their child or children.

'Looks like I'll be on my own after all,' she said, grinning, as it was almost our turn to go in.

'No, you can't,' I said. 'I'll explain the situation to the security guy. Either that or I'll stay with Jasmine while you go in and get what you need.'

'You will not!' Katie said. 'I don't leave her with no one, and I'll kick right off if you try and get this pram off me. You just watch me!'

Anxious not to create another huge scene, I waited till the security guard waved Katie in with the buggy, then immediately walked up to him to explain. I should have known how he'd react when he stuck a hand out towards my face. 'That's close enough, love,' he said. 'Two metres, remember?'

'I need to accompany her,' I said quietly, pointing to Katie's fast-disappearing back. 'I'm a foster carer and she can't be alone with that baby.'

To my utter consternation he laughed in my face. 'Trust me,' he said, 'I've heard every excuse going today, love. Rules are rules, and you're no different to anyone else, sorry.'

'I work for social services,' I said, trying to keep an even tone. 'And I am *required* to accompany that young lady and her baby.'

'What for?' he asked, loud enough to draw attention to himself, which I suspect he enjoyed, and to me, which I definitely didn't. 'Where's your bloody badge then?'

I gritted my teeth. I actually did have my social services ID card in my wallet, but there was no way I was going to carry this on any further. I was livid. Just then I saw the red stop light outside the store turn green. It was my turn to go in now in any case.

'Forget it,' I said icily. 'Oh, and thanks *so* much for your help!'

'Any time, lady, any time,' he retorted, with another stupid laugh.

Needless to say, by the time I was inside, I had lost Katie completely, and had no choice but to keep scurrying up and down along the ends of aisles to try and catch sight of her. It was almost 10 minutes before I finally tracked her down and by this time she was in a socially distanced till queue.

A glance into her basket revealed the things Katie had said she'd needed. Milk, a pack of nappies. Some baby wipes. A tube of barrier cream. All very innocent, granted. But from her animated face, once I'd got her attention, I had a feeling that some of her items may not have been so innocent. Or were not going to be paid for, from what I already knew of her. But short of accusing her and searching the pram, how could I know that for sure? In my heart I suspected that a quick dash to the booze section may well have happened, but other than keep an eye on her now, what else could I do?

'I thought you needed stuff,' she said, as I took up a spot the other side of the checkout. 'It's no worry. Me and Jasmine don't mind waiting for you.'

The checkout lady beamed. '*Such* a lovely name,' she cooed. 'And aren't you just the most *perfect* little *sweetheart*!' she added as she scanned Katie's shopping.

Katie didn't skip a single beat. Looking straight at me and with enough of a nod to leave zero room for doubt, she smiled right back at the checkout lady. 'She's named after my nan,' she said sweetly.

# Chapter 12

I went to bed that night feeling very uneasy, sure that there was more trouble ahead of us. Though Katie had been in a completely different frame of mind – affable, even – on the way back from the supermarket, I knew it was precisely because she thought she'd got one over on me. Though she managed not to actually smirk it was obvious that she'd found it highly amusing to both give me the runaround and take the mickey out of me in one fell swoop.

I also felt sure she had stolen some booze. And on that front, I really could have kicked myself. On the walk home I had decided that I would find some way to search the buggy covertly, though how I would manage that I didn't know. All I knew was that, given her minuscule handbag – a little boxy one with a gold chain, and barely room for a mobile and purse – whatever she'd pinched, if she had, would be hidden on it somewhere, just as Christine had warned me. So all I needed to do was separate her from it somehow, and I stood a good chance of laying my hands on any contraband. And, of course, she must have read my mind, because she duped me again.

We'd just turned into our road when she started up a huge commotion, flapping her hands and saying she'd seen a bee fly into the buggy and crawl under the baby's covers, and how it might sting her and that I needed to get it out – *now*.

'Are you sure?' I said, peering in and unable to see anything – not to mention thinking it unlikely that a bee, tootling around, getting nectar from spring flowers, would just land in a buggy and burrow underneath the blanket. It just didn't seem, well, very … *bee*-like.

'Please, Casey – will you just check for me? *Please*?? I'm terrified of bees – I got stung when I was little and my whole arm swelled up, and what if it stings Jaz? And she gets that anfilax-thingy? *Please*,' she said. 'I know it's in there somewhere. I *saw* it!'

Which, when I reflected on it later, was clever psychology. Because why would she let me pull the blanket off the buggy if she had something hidden in there she didn't want me to find? And somewhere in the middle of the kerfuffle, pulling off the cellular blanket that covered the baby and checking there was nothing to be seen, she plucked Jasmine up, and by some sleight of hand, while my attention was on the buggy, found a way to transfer whatever she'd taken from the shop to somewhere I definitely wouldn't think to look for it. I didn't know how, then. I only knew that, all of a sudden, the panic was over, she announced that it must have flown away again without us seeing, and she fairly skipped the rest of the way to our front gate.

'She's got a system,' I told Mike, once we were both tucked up in bed. 'She obviously *expected* me to search the buggy. To confront her about it. So she knew she'd have to find somewhere else to hide it before we got home. Even *among* the baby's clothes, I'm thinking.'

'Or – just a suggestion. I'm just playing devil's advocate here – a bee flew in the buggy and she was scared it would sting the baby?'

'I don't buy it. I've been done up like a kipper, Mike, I *know* it. All I don't know is where she hid it after that.'

'Up her jumper?' He grinned. 'Love, I'm serious. She could have shoved it up her jumper and there's nothing you can do about it. Well, short of ordering her to strip and/or ransacking her room. I think we have to accept that there is little we can do until something happens that we have to respond to. Which I imagine might happen tomorrow, as we can't stop her taking herself off and drinking it, either alone or with whoever she spent half the evening texting. She's probably planning some illegal gathering in the local park. And she won't be the first,' he added drily. 'Face it, love, with this one we're in fire-fighting mode. It's all we can be.'

I had to concede Mike was right. 'Well, at least she won't have baby with her if that's the case,' I said, 'and then if she does come back in a state, I'll just have to look after Jasmine myself until she sobers up. I'll have to write it all up in my reports though, so I might just mention that before she goes anywhere. Help concentrate her mind. She has to know that she's risking her whole future if she messes things up like this.'

Despite all the different possibilities and outcomes racing through my mind, I eventually nodded off, but the sleep must have been very fitful. I woke in the small hours, instantly alert, and knew I'd struggle to settle down again so, knowing from experience that it was better to have a glass of milk downstairs than toss and turn in bed, I pulled on my dressing gown and crept from the room, planning to potter around until I felt tired again.

I had just passed the bathroom when I heard what sounded like an argument coming from Katie's room. I frowned as I got closer because it was definitely getting louder; I had that sinking déjà vu feeling of having been here so many, many times before.

It was also clear that Katie was speaking to someone on either speakerphone or FaceTime, as I could hear a male voice shouting now too. I decided to knock on her door, albeit quietly because I didn't want to wake the baby (or, indeed Mike and Amelie) but Katie was obviously too engrossed in her spat to hear me. I tried again, but as it was obvious that an already heated argument was escalating further – a few choice profanities were being exchanged now – I decided to walk in.

I couldn't believe my eyes as I took in the entirety of the scene. Katie was in her bed, sitting propped up with pillows, and with her knees up in front of her. And, incredibly (or not so incredibly, to be honest, given the nature of my chosen career), little Jasmine was lying along her thighs, having her feed. And, similarly to baby Layla, who'd been with us so recently, she wasn't *being* fed; she was feeding herself. Not with her feet, but because Katie had propped up the bottle with a rolled-up towel, so it was at the right angle for the baby to suck on it, hands-free.

It was a dispiriting enough sight in itself, but made worse by the fact that the free hands in question were deployed by holding her mobile, and a bottle of spirits, respectively. So she *had* pinched some booze, and she *had* hidden it from me, but – and this was what upset me the most – she hadn't stolen it in anticipation of going off to some impromptu party. No, she was swigging it from the bottle, right under our noses, and while looking after her baby.

I felt anger mushroom up inside me. I was livid. But I was also in no mood for any kind of discussion right then. I really didn't trust myself not to lose my temper so I simply marched up to the bed and swiped the bottle from a stunned Katie's hand. 'End the call. Now!' I hissed. 'And then get that baby settled for the night. We will talk about this tomorrow. *Call*!' I added, as she drunkenly dithered about. 'End it! End it right now!'

Something about my tone, or perhaps my furious expression, must have stopped Katie from arguing with me. Though as the bottle – which contained vodka – was almost three-quarters empty, perhaps she was too befuddled to sufficiently gather her thoughts. She immediately told whoever it was that she had to go and hung up and, as I marched out of the room, was lifting up the baby and getting out of bed. Not a word was spoken between us, however, and I didn't look back. I didn't dare – I might have exploded.

I went downstairs and poured the remaining liquid down the sink before getting my own drink, which by now required a change from a glass of milk to a mug of coffee, because with the amount of adrenaline that was now pumping through me, I knew it would be quite a while before I felt sleepy again.

It was quite a while before my anger began to dissipate, as well. I had seen a lot of things in my lifetime and I'm far from being anywhere near perfect but to see that scene, that poor baby, so helpless, so vulnerable, so needing of care and love, yet having to suckle on a propped-up bottle – no loving arms, no soothing words, no precious bonding going on, while her mother – her entire *world* – screamed and swore down the phone to God knows who, while glugging on a bottle of bloody vodka!

It was just beyond me. I thanked God that at least Katie wasn't breastfeeding her baby, because the alcohol would surely have found its way into her milk. But that was only small consolation. What if she'd been so drunk that she'd fallen asleep with the baby laid like that? What if she'd rolled over and smothered her, or flipped her down onto the floor? Nine weeks in the world and already that tiny human being was being scandalously, heartbreakingly mistreated. That was a wake-up call in itself. I'd been given the impression that Katie had a drink problem, yes, but not that she was a danger to her little one. Yet, here she was, being exactly that.

I panicked then. What had I been thinking? Why on earth had I simply left her to it? Was she even capable enough to put Jasmine safely to bed? She could easily have just plonked her back in her cot on her front. And I didn't doubt for a moment that she wouldn't have winded her; so even if she had placed her on her back she could sick up a load of milk and choke on it. In short, I had messed up. Wouldn't the responsible thing have been to take the baby away from her?

I gulped down the last couple of mouthfuls of my coffee, turned the lights back off and crept back upstairs to listen outside Katie's room. I heard only silence now, but what did that prove? Clasping the door handle and moving as quietly as I could, I opened the door and crept back into the room.

Katie was already fast asleep, snoring softly in her bed, the glossy dark hair fanned out over the pillow and a sheen of sweat glistening on her forehead and upper lip. She would have one hell of a headache tomorrow, and that was even before the one I'd be giving her.

Jasmine, too, was sleeping, her tiny chest rising and falling reassuringly, flat on her back in the middle of the travel cot. So far so good, but, though relieved, I still wasn't entirely satisfied. So when I tiptoed back out again I left the bedroom door open, so I would be able to hear if Jasmine cried and Katie failed to get up to tend to her.

I left our room door open too, and eventually drifted back off to sleep, fatigue finally getting the upper hand over fury.

Which was not to say that I didn't wake the next morning still furious – a situation compounded by the fact that I'd had such a broken night and had – equally infuriatingly – woken up early.

Leaving Mike to sleep on, and with a check on Amelie confirming that she was doing likewise, I passed Katie's door, which was now closed, and headed downstairs. I needed fuel before embarking on the tedious post-mortem, and the likely arguments that I knew loomed ahead. I was shocked, though, to find that I wasn't alone. Mum and baby were already down in the kitchen, settling down on one end of the sofa, for a much more appropriate-looking feed.

It was just getting light and in the dull greyish gloom, Katie looked pretty grey too. She offered up a wan smile. 'I've just made you a coffee,' she said, somewhat sheepishly. 'I heard you in the bathroom when I came down, so I thought you'd been heading down here' –

she grimaced, then looked down at Jasmine – 'you know, to give me both barrels. It's on the counter there. I'm so sorry,' she added. 'Really. You've every right to give me hell.'

I picked up the mug. It smelled like coffee, certainly, but it didn't look at all like the way I normally had it. It was translucent-looking, lifeless and the colour of washing-up water. But it was the thought, right? It was a peace offering. I lifted it to my lips and sipped. It would do.

'I'm not going to give you hell, Katie. Partly because you're in the middle of feeding your lovely baby, and partly because it's not lost on me that it would be a monumental waste of time.'

I took my coffee and went to sit at the other end of the sofa. 'Katie, I'm sure you know only too well that I am obliged to record anything that happens while you're with us. Do you realise just how bad that looked last night?'

She nodded, and hung her head, unshed tears glistening in her eyes. 'I do,' she said. 'Honestly.' Then added, with some vehemence, 'It's just fucking *Josh*!' A tear slid down her cheek, which she wiped away angrily before it could plop onto the baby's face.

'Josh? As in …'

'My boyfriend. My dickhead of a boyfriend.'

Was this the young man the 'n'er-do-well' I'd been told about by Christine? I could only presume so.

'And why is Josh a "dickhead" of a boyfriend?'

'He's such a loser, Casey. And he's soooooo posses-sive. He wants to know where I am, what I'm doing, who I'm with, every bloody moment I'm away from him. So this' – she waved her free hand around the room to qualify what she meant by 'this' – 'has just sent him off on one. He got pissed last night and started accusing me of sleeping around with other lads, saying I'm fresh meat in a new town. All that kind of shit. I can't cope with it. I just … God, he's just *such* a loser.'

To which the logical response would have been to ask why, if that was the case, she didn't just finish with him. Why she didn't prioritise her baby, why she didn't do everything possible to ensure Jasmine wasn't taken away from her, including consigning the possessive (in my language 'dangerously controlling') boyfriend to history? Why? Why? *Why* didn't she do that? But I was too long in the tooth to be so reductionist and naive. The world was full of girls and women who stayed with men who mistreated and abused them. So it was the one question I wouldn't ask, because she already knew all those things. And had maybe even tried leaving him already. That she looked and sounded so genuinely upset made me think she might have, and possibly more than once. It was so easy to tell people life alone would be infinitely better than life with a toxic partner, but it wasn't something you *could* tell them. Not really. Not so they listened. It was one of those things people usually had to find out for themselves.

But still, jealous, controlling boyfriend woes or not, it didn't give Katie an excuse to get drunk and put such a young baby at risk. 'That's all well and good,' I said, 'and yes, I can understand you having a go at him if he's accusing you of such rubbish, especially given the complicated times we're all in. But how can you even conduct a relationship while we've all been confined to our homes? Does Josh pre-date the pandemic?' I asked, since I realised I had no idea who the baby's father was. Katie nodded. 'But Jasmine's not his?'

Now she shook her head. 'We split up, couple of years back.' So this really was a teen romance, I thought. 'I, you know, got with someone … and, well, got myself pregnant. We got back together once I was already four months gone.' She nodded down towards the baby, who had by now finished feeding; looked milk-drunk, in fact, her tummy nice and full, and her eyes flickering closed, pulling her back to the tranquillity of sleep. No tranquillity in her future, by the sound of it though, not with her mum in a dysfunctional relationship with a young man who wasn't her father. I felt my anger bubble up again.

'And how did Josh feel about all that?'

I saw Katie stiffen. 'He wanted to get back with me, didn't he?'

But the idea of parenting a child and the reality were very different. Even with the best will in the world, and I didn't imagine much of that was in play in this case. I started formulating my next question, which was how he felt about it *now*, about the baby that wasn't his, as opposed to then. But I stopped myself. This wasn't my foster child (and to me, then, she felt very much like a child still), and not my business to delve into.

'And how about you?' I asked instead. 'Katie, you know full well that downing the best part of a bottle of spirits when you have a baby daughter to look after is just not acceptable. I shouldn't need to tell you that.'

'I know,' she said, her voice contrite now rather than petulant. 'And I'm so, so sorry. It won't happen again, I promise. He just stressed me out so much … and, you know, it was there, and I just … Well, I just reached for it …'

'And *how* was it there?' I asked, back on territory that *was* mine. 'Did you buy it in the supermarket yesterday?'

For a moment, I could see her considering how to respond. Working out whether to be honest, or plead innocence. After all, she was 18. Legally an adult. She could have brought it with her, and was free to drink as much vodka as she pleased. But, to her credit, she came clean. She nodded.

'And where did you hide it?' I asked. 'I'm assuming all the bee nonsense was staged so you could secrete it somewhere?'

'Just down my trackies,' she said, as if that was the sort of thing everyone did as a matter of course. 'Look, I *know* I drink too much, and I know I've got to get my shit together. And I will.' She lifted up the baby and

151

cuddled her into her chest, and began patting her back to wind her, with undeniable tenderness. There were still tears shining in her eyes, and I decided to let it go. With the hangover she must have had, she was clearly suffering enough.

Plus, it wasn't for me to get too involved. The relationship with the boy would either go down in flames or not, and the same applied to whether she got to keep her baby. There was little I could do, and little that I should do, aside from reporting any incidents. Which I would do. I'd have to. But Katie wasn't my problem. Not a nice thing to acknowledge, but nevertheless the truth. I also trusted my fellow carer to do all she could to reach the right outcome. In the meantime, I could only hope the girl had learned a lesson.

And it seemed she might have. Because the rest of the day was harmonious and peaceful. Amelie was, of course, simply besotted with baby Jasmine, so Katie didn't have to do much, and was able to nurse her hangover – mostly by curling up on the sofa and scrolling endlessly through her phone while Amelie giggled and fussed over her daughter. Luckily, being so young, the baby slept a lot anyway, so I wasn't worried about Amelie spending all her time with her.

I had to laugh though, when my mum FaceTimed me later in the afternoon, because when it was Amelie's turn to chat, she said, 'Oh, Nannie, I'd love to spend ages with you, but my baby keeps me so busy I don't really have the time. I got to go sort her bed out so it's cosy for when she sleeps, and then I got to sing to her and help do bottles. Honestly, Nannie, I'm shattered!'

'Well, dear,' my mum said, managing a quick wink at me, 'it sounds like you have your hands full! I'd best let you get on then, and I'll speak to you tomorrow.'

Though I laughed as I closed the laptop, I felt the usual pang of guilt. Yes, we were all in the same boat – not just the country but the entire planet – but it felt all wrong that I was hunkered down with three girls I wasn't related to, and couldn't even hug my own mum.

There might, it seemed however, be some news on the horizon, because as I put away the laptop I could feel my phone vibrating in my pocket. It was Christine, with an update on Amelie. Though I knew Christine worked all hours, it was still unusual to hear from her on a Saturday, so perhaps she had something good to impart.

Leaving Amelie assisting Katie with Jasmine's umpteenth nappy change of the day, I headed out into the garden to take the call.

'Sorry to disturb you guys on a weekend,' Christine said, 'but I thought you'd want to hear my news straight away. First up, we've located Amelie's father.'

'Oh wow!' I said. 'That's great news. Well, I hope it is. Or isn't it? That doesn't sound like a very good news voice.'

'Because it isn't, not really,' she said. 'He doesn't think he can help. He lives miles away now, and works as a hospital porter. He's engaged to a nurse from the hospital he works at, and because of the danger their jobs potentially put them in, given Covid, he believes it's just not the right time to be considering taking on a long-lost daughter.'

'Oh,' I said, and then had another thought. 'But when the pandemic is over? What about then?'

'Well, that's the thing, Casey,' Christine said. 'I did ask that exact question, and you know, I think that it's simply because he doesn't want to take her on at all. He was obviously just making excuses – not that he needs to, to be honest. He split up with Mum – and it was she that ended it – not long after Amelie was born. He barely even knew her. He started blustering a bit then, saying he wasn't sure he was the right person, and that he felt it would be in Amelie's best interests to have a completely fresh start in any case.'

'Right,' I said, flatly. 'With complete strangers as opposed to an actual parent. Yes, I'm sure that's in her best interests.'

There was a pause. Then Christine said, 'Bit of a bad day?'

Her voice was instantly sympathetic. Which made me feel bad. 'Oh, don't mind me,' I said. 'I don't mean to sound snippy. Just a bit of a broken night, that's all. You know how it goes. Anyway,' I rattled on, not wanting to go over all the Katie stuff right now. It was her weekend too, after all. That could wait till Monday. 'So we're still where we were then. Full care order. Adoptive parents …'

'Actually, at least potentially, that's not set in stone anymore.'

'How so?'

'That's my other bit of news and this bit is potentially much more positive. An aunt has appeared, would you believe? And seemingly out of the blue. Well, I say out of the blue, but actually by way of social media. Facebook of all things. It's Kelly's sister, name of Robyn. She found out through friends of friends about the house fire just a few days ago. The sisters have been estranged since Amelie was around two. I don't know all the ins and outs yet, but we're going to chat again early next week. It took her until yesterday to establish all the facts and to find out that Amelie was in care. Anyway, long story short, the woman wants to see her niece. She's asked for a window visit.'

'That *is* good news,' I said. 'So, is this aunt considering taking on Amelie then?'

'*Very* early days yet,' Christine said, 'but I'm cautiously optimistic. She's got this far, after all, which to my mind means she's given things pretty serious consideration. She could equally as well not come forward, couldn't she? Now, whether this is out of sympathy, or curiosity, or just on principle – trying to do the right thing, wanting to step up – I'm looking on it as a positive. As is the fact that she is single – just out of a longish relationship – and has no children of her own. I get the impression she saw quite a lot of them before the sisters fell out. Of course, she might not want to take on Amelie in the permanent legal guardianship sense, but who knows? She took the time to track us down, and wants to meet her niece, and to me that speaks volumes. She wouldn't want to see the child if she didn't plan on having *some* involvement in her future life, would she?'

Christine was right. You'd have to be a very strange person to actively seek out the child and ask to meet her if you hadn't at least considered the possibility of playing some part in her future life. To do otherwise would just be so cruel.

We didn't have any chickens, so I couldn't count any, obviously. And nor would I. But as I went back inside, and saw Amelie down on the floor singing to the baby, the very picture of joy and innocence, I allowed myself the luxury of at least hoping.

# Chapter 13

It was such a lift getting that news from Christine, and I felt a stirring of real positivity, but I was wary about telling Amelie about it for obvious reasons, so Mike and I decided not to tell her anything until there was something definite to impart.

'No point introducing the idea of a long-lost aunt in case the woman has second thoughts or something,' Mike said, 'and definitely no point mentioning anything about her father, not now he's made his intentions, or lack of them, clear.'

He was right of course, and I bristled at the thought of what Amelie's dad had said. I understood his reasoning, as much as I felt sad about it, but the thought of reuniting with a daughter he hadn't seen for years, and barely knew, just after he'd got engaged and was set to get married must have been a pretty daunting prospect. Sadly, it was an all too common occurrence in my world and it didn't do to dwell on it. These things happened.

Still, it would have been nice if some form of contact could have been arranged just so that Amelie could place him in her life. And who knew? Now he knew of her situation, maybe he'd have second thoughts about it himself. The girl was his flesh and blood, after all. For now, though, I had to focus on the happy possibility that Aunt Robyn might make good on her promise to be involved in some way.

The day continued towards teatime with the positive vibe, and it was lovely to see Katie allowing Amelie to help out the way she did, and if I'm honest, it gave me a bit of a breather. I hadn't realised until now just how much one-to-one time we'd had to spend with Amelie, and how exhausted I'd actually been. Having Katie there gave me some much-needed time to just sit and do nothing, and make the most of the beautiful weather we'd been having.

'Guess what, Casey, go on, just guess!' Amelie yelled as she ran out to the garden just before I was about to go in and start on making tea.

'I can't guess,' I replied, laughing. 'You'll just have to tell me.'

'I'm allowed to help Katie *actually* bath the baby. I mean like proper help, like use the sponge to wipe the bubbles off and everything, and I can even sprinkle some baby powder on her little arms and legs afterwards. I'm so excited! Aren't you?'

'I am indeed excited,' I said, 'but remember you have to be very careful, because she's very tiny, so don't be too excitable. You have to be very calm and gentle with her, okay?'

'I will, I promise. I pinky promise,' Amelie said, holding up her little finger to entwine it with mine. A pinky promise was a solemn vow that could never be broken; something we had established together the previous day.

And so the positive vibes continued. There wasn't even any tension at the dinner table as I served up a homemade quiche and a salad. In fact, it was really convivial, with everyone laughing and chatting about the day, and Katie in fits of giggles at Mike's awful dad jokes.

'Is it okay if I go upstairs with Katie to help bath Jasmine now?' Amelie asked as Katie reached into the pram to pick her daughter back up.

I glanced at Katie, who looked a bit tired, I thought. Did she really want to go to all the hassle of bathing Jasmine tonight? It could equally wait till the morning, before they left us. 'Well, I'm not sure Jasmine actually *needs* a bath tonight, to be honest. How about you wait till tomorrow and –'

But Katie was already nodding. 'It's fine,' she said, ruffling Amelie's hair with her free hand. 'She's a good little helper, actually, and I did promise.'

What could I say to that? Nothing really, other than to remind both girls not to take too long, as it would soon be time for Amelie to have a bath and get ready for bed too.

'Maybe this weekend is going to be a breeze,' Mike said, as he stacked the plates and left the table, before catching up on the daily news on TV. 'And it's actually giving us a break too, from our little whirlwind.'

He wasn't wrong, and it reminded me just how hands-on he was every day with Amelie. There was barely a moment when one or other of us wasn't entertaining her in some way. And she patently adored him. But I wasn't sure about the word 'breeze'. In my experience, in my world, 'breezes' didn't generally last too long, and I wasn't going to tempt fate by letting my guard down.

And I was right not to. A big-up to my feminine intuition, I thought, because just an hour after I'd settled Amelie down for the night, Katie reappeared in the living room with a sheepish look on her face.

'Would you guys mind just listening out for Jasmine for me for an hour? She's been fed and changed and is sleeping so she shouldn't wake up, but I've left the door open so you can hear if she cries.'

'You off to have a nice bath, love?' I asked, immediately realising that was a pretty stupid question, as Katie had changed her clothes and also donned a face-full of make-up.

'Um, no,' she said, her eyes flicking downwards rather than meeting mine. 'I've decided to make the most of it and go out for my hour's exercise,' she said. 'I mean, it's still not that late, and it's not dark, and I didn't think you'd mind.' Her eyes met mine now. 'Not after me entertaining Amelie for most of the day. I just need to get out for a bit now.'

I glanced at Mike, who was sitting on the sofa scrolling through channels. No, it wasn't that late, but it was later than I was strictly comfortable with. I was also a bit annoyed about her throwing a tit-for-tat card in. But there was little I could do, bar blankly refusing. And she *was* allowed out, and she wasn't allowed to take the baby with her. A *fait accompli*, then. I glanced at the clock.

'That's fine then,' I finally said. 'If you really need to get out then do it. Go stretch your legs. But Katie, it's 7.00 p.m., and you know the rules. One hour. So you have until 8.00 p.m., 8.10 at the very latest,' I added, to display a bit of good faith. 'Do you understand? Eight ten and no later.'

Katie nodded and assured me she would be back on time, then left. I didn't like it, not after the events of the previous night, but there was nothing I could have done differently anyway. As she couldn't leave the house alone with the baby, it was my job and my duty to look after Jasmine if she wanted to take her hour of exercise, and there was nothing to say she couldn't, as long as she followed the government guidelines. Still, I felt that all-too-familiar sense of unease, and that nagging feeling I got when I knew something was going on but I simply couldn't put my finger on what it was.

I didn't voice my fears to Mike though, and in fact took some solace that he seemed quite unfazed by the whole thing. 'She's 18, love,' was his only comment.

'And she's not our foster kid, remember? We provide bed and board and we follow the rules. So chill out, okay?'

He was right. So, leaving him to watch the undercover cop programme he'd finally selected, I announced that I would go sort our wardrobes out.

'I've been putting it off for weeks,' I said, 'so I might as well go make a start and I can check in on the baby while I'm up there. Better to be occupied than sit and watch the clock.'

Needless to say, knee-deep in old clothes and charity bags, the hour whizzed round to eight pretty quickly. Then 8.10, then 8.15, and though the baby was still sleeping soundly, I was irritable. Much as I half-expected a bit of pushback from a teenager, I felt let down that *this* teenager, already on such shaky ground, had thrown my faith in her back in my face. I went back downstairs and paced the floor while ranting to Mike.

'I just can't believe it,' I said, having by now tried her phone, only to find it was switched off. Of course it was. 'See, this is what you get for trusting someone. I mean, how long do we give her before calling it in?' I looked at the clock yet again. 'I mean, even if she comes in now, we read her the riot act, right? It's bloody 25 past already!'

Mike, no longer unfazed of course, had started to look stressed. Probably more from anticipating me being on the war path than about Katie herself. 'I don't know, Case, it's not like she's a young kid. She's in the wrong, yes, but look, let's give her till 8.45. If she's still not back by then, yes, we report it to EDT. And if she *is* back, you still report it in your notes. She was told what we expected and she's blatantly disregarded it, so she's only got herself to blame, hasn't she?'

When Katie wasn't back at 8.55 I made a decision. 'Right then. It's not just EDT, Mike, it's got to be the police too, because she's in our care regardless of her age. She's breaking the Covid laws now too. And, strictly speaking, she has also abandoned her baby. But before I ring anyone, I wonder if you shouldn't just have a quick drive around the block, just in case you can see her? She might have lost track of time, and she might have even got lost, but either way a quick ride around won't take long, will it? And if you don't find her, then I'll make the calls.'

Perhaps because it gave him a legitimate excuse to leave the house, Mike agreed. He quickly swapped slippers for trainers and grabbed his car keys. 'Best make some coffee, Case,' he said as he left. 'Could be a long bloody night, this.'

I could only wait then, and pray that he did find her. I didn't know quite why I was so intent on giving her second chances. Perhaps it was the knowledge that she was in a toxic relationship and that I didn't doubt the no-good boyfriend was pulling her strings. And if Mike *did* find her, I just had to hope that a reprimand and a mention in my notes would be enough to make her think twice about doing it again. So when I heard the front door opening only a few minutes later, I sent a silent prayer to the gods. He must have found her, or he wouldn't have returned home so quickly.

My bubble of relief was immediately burst. 'You won't bloody believe it!' Mike said, stomping into the living room. 'Casey, you're going to have to deal with this one, I'm afraid.'

'Why? What the hell's going on?' I asked. 'Have you found her or not?'

'Oh, I've found her alright,' he said, clearly fuming. 'She's up the bloody road, just inside the entrance to the park. On a bench, and practically having sex with some young toerag. Saints alive,' he growled. 'And doing it only two minutes away from the bloody house!'

'Did she see you?' I asked, quickly grabbing a cardigan from the dining chair back, 'Did you say anything to them?'

'No, Casey, I didn't,' he said, throwing his car keys down on the counter. 'If I'd have got out of the car, I just don't know what I might have said or done. The bloody brazen way they were carrying on! And there are people out, walking their bloody dogs! But trust me, we are the last thing on her mind right now. Oh, and she sounds like she's off her head too. I could hear her giggling and screeching from the car. Trust me, you are the best one to deal with this. I'd probably end up in a row with the lad.'

Leaving my own feet in my slippers – I wouldn't be going far, after all – I set off up the road. It was just getting dark now, a chill in the air, and the street lamps had just started coming on. I ran up to where Mike had told me to go, a park that I took my little grandkids to regularly – well, at least before Covid, I did – and not somewhere unruly teens generally gathered. But these were not normal times and as I approached, I could hear distant but unmistakeable sounds of youthful revelry. Not surprising really. It was getting increasingly hard for everyone to keep youngsters in.

Katie and Josh – assuming it was Josh – were not part of that, though. As Mike had described they were on, no, *behind*, one of the benches near the entrance. As soon as I was in earshot, I shouted her name. It was the boy who reacted first, and he acted immediately, practically shoving Katie over the wall they'd been leaning against in his haste to get over it himself, and take off at speed, which, of course, he duly did.

By the time I got there, she was back on her feet and adjusting her top, giggling. And once again, I could see she'd been drinking. 'Shozz,' she said. 'Dint r'lise the time.' She was swaying. She could hardly keep herself upright. What was it with stupid kids and necking neat spirits?

'What the bloody hell do you think you're doing?' I yelled at her. I couldn't stop myself. 'God, look at the state of you! And who was that?'

'Thashh Josh,' she slurred, still giggling. 'He'sh my boyfriend ... He's cute, ishenee?' Then she promptly vomited, almost projectile-vomited, covering both herself, the back of the bench and my slippers. 'Oopsh,' she said once she was done, wiping a hand over her mouth.

I could have cried. Not just because of the state she was in, but now my bloody favourite slippers were covered in sick. It had also, I noticed, splashed all up my legs. It smelt vile. There was absolutely no point in being confrontational, however, not while she was like this, no point in trying to have a conversation about her lack of responsibility, or about forgetting she had a time limit, or forgetting she had a bloody baby, for that matter. So instead, I put an arm around her and used the other one to hold her up.

'Come on, Katie,' I said wearily, 'let's get you home and showered. Then bed. You have a lot to sleep off.'

'I do!' she said, weaving about as we made our way out of the park. 'I need my bed. Thash 'xaclly what we need!'

Oh, there was a lot more vomiting done that night. I first had to strip her down, hold her in the shower, and try my best to get some pyjamas on her. She was a lot bigger than me so this was no mean feat in itself, and obviously, Mike couldn't help me. Her drunken babble, of which there was a fairly constant stream, told me that Josh, the jealous boyfriend, had arranged this little meet-up, and that he'd brought her a bottle of vodka as a present. (*Nothing like being in a relationship where you both become the best people you can be*, I thought wryly.) She'd drunk almost all of it, too. So there was no way she was fit to look after the baby that night (she was still vomiting at gone midnight) and we had to bring Jasmine's carry cot into our room, and I had to deal with both night feeds. Not only that, but I was so afraid that Katie might choke on her own vomit that I was in and out of her room all night checking on her too. It was a nightmare, and I think I slept twice, for about 20 minutes each time, before finally resigning myself to the fact that I may as well just forget I had a bed that night.

I didn't have much of a chance to speak with Katie the next morning either, as she didn't wake until 9.00 a.m. and was being collected at 10.00 a.m. But I did go into her room as she was feeding Jasmine, after dressing her, having asked Mike to take Amelie off to – ironically – the park, to feed the ducks to keep her out of the way. About which she'd pouted a little, but since I'd let her help me change and dress Jasmine at 7.30 'while Mummy Katie had a lie-in', she soon got over herself.

'So, last night?' I asked Mummy Katie now, standing in her doorway, hands on hips.

'I know. I fucked up big time again, didn't I?' she said. She looked awful. She must have felt awful, but my sympathy was now in short supply. 'I'm so, so sorry,' she finished. 'Did you report me?'

'You did,' I said. 'And, as you say, big time. And if you mean to EDT and the police, no, I didn't. But I could have. I have, however, written it up in my notes. I had no choice, Katie, and I think you know that. I honestly don't know what will happen now, and I feel for you and Jasmine, but that's down to your social worker now and the courts.'

We barely had time to talk further, as she still needed to shower and dress, and it was with a deep sense of sadness that I watched her tearfully climb into the car an hour later, hugging Jasmine before handing her over to the social worker, who strapped her into the car seat. Did she see it the way I was seeing it? As a dry run for the day when the social worker would be doing exactly that, except Katie would not be going with them?

Thank goodness Amelie didn't understand what was happening, at least. Indeed, as they drove away and she finally finished her frantic waving, having returned just before they left, she said, 'That was the funnest weekend in my life! Oh, I can't wait for them to come again. Will it be soon?'

Mike smiled down at her. 'You never know, kiddo,' he said as he picked her up and positioned her on his hip. 'But I'm sure there'll be other kids coming along soon and you'll have new friends to meet. And maybe even school. How about that, then? And in the meantime, you and me have some digging to do.'

And off they went to the back garden to start creating a wildflower patch for Amelie, leaving me to make a very uncomfortable phone call to Christine, who would by now have already picked up my urgent email. Having written it all down, it was starkly obvious: Katie had broken pretty much every rule she could. There was little question. Her future was probably now sealed.

# Chapter 14

After our whirlwind weekend with Katie, and all the emotion it had stirred up in everyone (me especially), it was a relief to settle back into our harmonious little threesome. And though Amelie asked me regularly when they were going to 'deliver another baby', she showed a surprising degree of pragmatism about all the comings and goings and abrupt changes to her routine. Well, surprising until you realised that it was probably a function of her chaotic upbringing; having known so little stability in her young life up till now, perhaps there was very little that would unsettle or surprise her.

I was also holding on, very tightly, to the idea of Robyn, who, despite my vowing to myself not to get any hopes up, had become, in my mind, a fully realised fairy godmother, ready to swoop in and offer Amelie a whole new life. I knew she could have a good life with *any* loving adoptive parents, but I still nurtured the belief that if a similarly loving blood relative took her on, that would be the best outcome of all, because, despite the chaotic nature of her early life, I felt strongly that her aunt would be in the best possible position to keep a loving memory of her mother alive.

Of Kelly herself, I thought very little. There had been no further update, and no requests for further contact, and with preparations for the care order going on behind the scenes, I imagined we'd hear very little more from her.

So my very last thought, when my phone went at 2 a.m. a few nights later, was that she might still have some fixation about *me*.

It was a warm night, one of many we'd had recently, and Mike had rigged up a fan close to the bed. So when I first woke, I thought it had been the whirring noise that had woken me, only realising it was my phone from the glow on the bedside table.

I leaned over groggily, to see No Caller ID. EDT, then, and my first thought was that I was highly tempted to ignore it. After all, we had already been doing our bit. But that was quickly replaced by two stronger emotions. A sense of responsibility – someone must need us – and, of course, good old curiosity.

I pulled the phone from the charger and swiped to accept the call, whispering my 'hello' so I wouldn't wake Mike.

'You fucking bitch!' a female voice said, in a furious hiss rather than a whisper. 'You think they're not watching you and reporting back to me?'

'Um … er … what?' I responded, still groggy from sleep.

'They've got eyes and ears *everywhere*, and they are coming for you, bitch!'

I pulled back the duvet, got out of bed, and padded out onto the landing. 'Kelly?' I asked, not so much recognising the voice as the content. 'Is that Kelly? And how do you have this number? And why on *earth* –'

'I have *everything*,' she responded, as I slipped into the bathroom.

'Why on *earth*,' I finished, 'are you calling me at this hour?'

'I see you,' she went on. 'I know what you're up to. I have eyes and ears everywhere and I know what you're up to. Don't think you'll get away with your plots and your evil. There are many, many, many ways to swing a cat. You think you're so clever, but –'

'Kelly, are you on your own?' I asked, my brain at last fully functioning. She was obviously in the middle of having some sort of episode. 'Is there anyone there with you? Someone you can call?'

'Don't fucking interrupt me! *Listen*! Just fucking listen! I have eyes and ears everywhere. I have eyes and ears *everywhere*. I have –'

'Kelly, where are you? Are you in the hospital? You need to call someone. You –'

'*No, you* need to call. *You* need to call someone. I have eyes and ears everywhere. Just you fucking believe it. You think you call the shots, bitch, but *I* call the shots.

If you don't, right this *minute*, make' – the next bit was indecipherable, her voice increasing in pitch and speed and volume – 'and the ghosts of the past will – the harbingers of *evil* …' Another incoherent string of words then ensued. But one word I did pick up on, and more than once, was 'knives'.

'Kelly!' I tried, now adopting a stern, snappy tone, and hoping that her increasingly loud utterances would alert someone nearby. Though, in truth I had no idea where she even was. Was she still in the hospital? Or had they discharged her? Either way, this conversation was futile. Futile and, come to that, scary. 'Kelly,' I said again, 'I'm going to end the call now, okay. You have to –' But the call suddenly ended in any case.

I stood in the bathroom for a few minutes, watching a moth skitter across the window pane. Where on earth had Amelie's mum got my number? I was shocked. Tight security around carers' personal details was sacrosanct, always. As it would be, and should be, for good reason.

I opened the window wider to allow the moth to make its escape, then padded back into the bedroom and slipped into bed. But I was obviously not as fully awake now as I'd thought (or perhaps just too discombobulated) because just as I was finally drifting back off to sleep, my mobile rang again. Why on earth had I not thought to put the bloody ringer on silent?

This time Mike did wake. 'Wha …? What's going on? Who the hell's that?' he mumbled groggily.

'No one,' I whispered, as I declined to take the call. Then I turned the ringer off, holding the side of the phone close to the digital clock display to double-check that I'd done so. 'Go back to sleep, love,' I said, turning the mobile onto its front for good measure. 'Just a text.' And a phone call to be made first thing in the morning. How on *earth* had she managed to get my number?

'I have absolutely no idea,' Christine admitted, once I got through to her at one minute past nine the following morning, with details of my nocturnal verbal assault. Part of me, by this time, felt sorry for the poor woman. To be in the grip of a horrible mental illness must be a terrifying thing. And, though her words had been angry, her voice had held something else that suggested that too: genuine fear. And it hadn't just been the two calls, either. There had been a further six – three close together an hour after the first two, and then three further calls, spaced out at intervals, the last coming at around four thirty, when, thankfully, I was obviously fast asleep. But though I was concerned for her – hadn't she been doing well? Hadn't she been stabilised by her treatment? – part of me felt anxious for *our* safety as well. If she'd managed to get my number, what else had she found out about us?

'Well, she clearly found a way,' I said. 'Which makes me wonder. Is she even still in hospital? And if they *have* discharged her, wouldn't they have informed you?'

'Not necessarily,' Christine said. 'Everything is so up in the air right now, and so many people are working from home, that the collective left hand often seems not to know what the collective right hand is doing. And, besides, I don't think the hospital has any legal requirement to share information about their patients with us. Not until such time as it becomes necessary for them to do so, anyway. And it could be that she was only discharged in the last couple of days. Maybe the information simply hasn't filtered through yet.'

'Or she's escaped …' I suggested, thinking out loud more than anything.

'I very much doubt that,' Christine said. 'It's a secure facility. And if she's had some sort of relapse, they'd be monitoring her closely. Anyway, sit tight. I'll make some calls and get back to you. But if you hear any more from her, of course let me know.'

As I'd half expected, my phone remained silent all morning, and as we set about some online school work the local primary had sent for Amelie the previous day, my principal feeling was that this was all further evidence that we were going down the right road. If Kelly's mental health was that unstable even with all the professional help she was getting there was no way she should have any further contact with Amelie. All these weeks on, in our bright, sunny lockdown existence, it was all too easy to forget that on the night she'd burnt the family home down, it was only Amelie's actions that had saved both their lives. It seemed incredible, in fact, that they hadn't both died.

But Kelly was, it seemed, very much still in hospital.

'And very much,' Christine said when she called back at lunchtime, 'still undergoing treatment.' Confidentiality laws meant she was unable to give me a great deal of detail on Kelly's current condition, at least much beyond '*un*stable', but she had been able to establish the chain of events that ended with Kelly in possession of my mobile number.

Which was unsettling enough in itself. 'It was a Post-it note,' she explained. 'One of the nurses at the facility wrote your number down on one to be input into an iPad for the FaceTime call Kelly had with Amelie the other week. Then, without thinking, she'd left it stuck to some paperwork on the table, and another member of staff had scrunched it up and put it in the bin.'

'And Kelly had clocked that?'

'Indeed she had,' Christine said. 'And had retrieved the Post-it note later, waiting for an opportunity to put it to use.'

'Wow,' I said. 'What must have been going through her mind?'

'That you had become part of the bigger picture of her conspiracy theories, I imagine. Either that, or she hoped to get back in touch with Amelie, I suppose. But why would she do that when she could simply ask for another FaceTime? Plus, from what you say she said to you, I'd suggest it's the former rather than the latter, don't you think? Anyway, her opportunity came a couple of days ago when a new patient arrived at the facility and, being something of a regular, this girl apparently knew all the tricks and had managed to sneak a mobile past Security.'

'So much for the "secure facility" then,' I commented dryly.

'Touché,' she said, with a wry chuckle. 'But don't forget there are *whole drug gangs* running even inside Category A prisons. Anyway, it seems Kelly managed to talk the girl into letting her have the phone overnight last night, and, well, there you go. It's been confiscated now, of course, and they even manged to find the Post-it note slipped beneath Kelly's mattress, so they assure me it won't – can't – happen again.'

Except it could, of course. I knew nothing of the set-up there, but, as Christine had pointed out, people tended to find ways around restrictive systems. Who wasn't to say Kelly wouldn't find a way to do so a second time?

# Chapter 15

I kept my phone on silent every bedtime for the follow-ing three days, just in case, but, thankfully, there were no more calls from Amelie's mother. And by the end of the week I had gone from being a bit spooked and nervous to just feeling sad for the poor woman. However threatening she had sounded, I kept coming back to the mental state that had prompted the calls. To have such terrifying thoughts about the world around you swirling inside your head twenty-four seven must be a living hell. She was frightened and had lashed out in the same way an animal would if it was trapped and unable to escape. As someone who was fortunate enough to take my sanity almost for granted, I could only count my blessings.

Still, the continued restrictions of our own lockdown lives were beginning to take their toll. We weren't exactly climbing the walls (we had the luxury of a garden, after all, which many didn't) but, like everyone else, we were human animals, and human animals craved the company of others, novelty, stimulation, and even the delights of the hot tub and our early veg crops were beginning to pall.

Which meant the news that the prime minister was soon to make an announcement about restrictions couldn't have come soon enough. It was almost June, and it felt like we'd been locked down forever, so when the announcement duly came that afternoon, that we were going to be able to meet up with others in the privacy of our own gardens, no less, it felt just like Christmas was around the corner.

Yes, there would be conditions, talks of 'bubbles', '2-metre distancing' and the 'rule of six' and so on, but it meant that I could have Mum and Dad round at last. Which of course meant we had to have them over for a barbecue. We'd invite my sister Donna, too, since she was very down, and also anxious, about having had to close her little tearoom (her business and sole livelihood), and though I was sad that that left no room for my own children and grandkids, it at least meant that I wouldn't have to invite some and not others, which would be hugely distressing in itself. Plus, with the first day of the new rules being a Monday, in any case, most of ours wouldn't be able to come anyway, since all of them, in some fashion or other, were still working. Hopefully in not too long we could *all* get together, and in the meantime, Mum and Dad would, I knew, be thrilled.

Having called Mum and Dad, I immediately hit upon a potential snag. Wouldn't half of Britain be thinking exactly the same thing as I was? Yes, the early shortages had settled (there was only so much loo roll every household would stockpile, after all) but there would no doubt be a massive rush on anything that was barbecue-related.

'How do you fancy a trip to the supermarket?' I asked Mike the following morning. Not usually his area, but I knew he'd enjoy getting out of the house.

'And me!' Amelie trilled. 'And me! Can I be your helper?'

He had just opened his mouth to answer when she immediately hurried on. 'I promise I'll be good, I know all the shopping rules.'

'Shopping rules?' he asked her. Then twigged what she was on about. 'That's okay, kiddo. Children don't have to wear masks, only grown-ups.'

Now Amelie looked confused. 'No, the cameras,' she said. 'I know I mustn't look at the cameras. And I know I mustn't say anything in case they hear me.'

'Cameras?' I asked.

'The FBI cameras,' she qualified. 'So the bad mens don't know we're there. They *watch*,' she added, as if imparting a state secret. 'And they listen to everything and *everyone*. But I know the rules. So they won't know that *we're* there.'

It felt a little ironic that what she said was, in fact, true. Even the supermarket loyalty card was well known for being in the data collection business, for goodness' sake. And I knew full well that my mate Alexa was always listening in too. Not to mention our smartphones.

Yet the picture Amelie painted, just like the others, was still unsettling – I visualised her and her mum scuttling round Tesco, heads down, anxious, feeling vulnerable. It must surely affect Amelie's feelings about the outside world.

'Amelie,' I said, gently, 'yes, of course you can go to the supermarket with Mike, and we know you'll be a good girl, but there really are no systems watching and listening to us in there for any "bad mens". Yes, they do have cameras, so they can see if someone's doing something they shouldn't be. But the FBI aren't spying on anyone. In fact, the FBI are part of the police force in America – which is a whole other country, on the other side of the *world*, so –'

'But they have eyes and ears *everywhere*,' she finished for me, echoing her mother's hissed words of a few nights previously. I changed tack. 'You know what,' I said, 'there is something I should explain to you. The whole story about the bad men and the FBI watching everyone in the shops – I think it might have been Mummy who told you that, right?' She nodded. 'Well, I think she was just playing an exciting game of make-believe with you so you wouldn't get bored when you were out doing the shopping.'

She considered me for a moment, with those big trusting eyes of hers. 'So it wasn't real?'

'No, sweetie. I think it was just a game. To make things more fun, more exciting. You have nothing to worry about when you go out, okay?'

She didn't look convinced. And why would she be? It probably didn't feel much like a game, not when your mum was transmitting so much fear and anxiety, as she almost certainly would have been. But Amelie was a child and couldn't help but live mostly in the moment, and right now she was excited about organising our little garden party.

'Okay,' she said, as if to shut down that line of chat in any case. 'Are we going to buy balloons?'

Half an hour later, armed with a comprehensive list of everything we could pick up in advance, I was waving the pair of them off to join what would probably be the monster queue snaking around the local supermarket. And though I smiled as I watched them go, a part of me felt sad. I knew what Kelly's mum had was a serious and often lifelong condition, and it struck me that chronic mental illness didn't just affect the sufferer. It rippled out and affected everyone in that person's orbit, making casualties of other people also. It seemed such a shame that Kelly hadn't got the help she'd clearly needed much sooner, and in doing so alerted those who needed to know about Amelie, so they could have got the support they needed, because its impact on her had been profound. In her world, her mother had been the be-all and end-all, and she'd had no reason to ever not believe everything she'd been told. It must now be so confusing for her to have another, supposedly trusted, adult turn everything she thought she knew on its head.

I guessed all I could do was keep chipping away. No big fuss, and no conflicts; just quietly replacing one set of beliefs about things with another via reinforcement, and hopefully beginning to overlay what had gone before.

In the meantime the house was suddenly very quiet. It was mid-morning on a Thursday, the cleaning had been done, and Mike and Amelie would be gone for at least an hour. So an ideal opportunity to make some phone calls. First on my list was Christine, who'd texted earlier, saying she'd like to give me a catch-up on the school situation once I had a moment. So I settled down with a coffee and made the call.

'I've got you a visit at the school,' she said. 'From Monday they are allowing certain children to return on a rotating basis. Reception, Year 1, and Year 6, at the moment. I think Amelie, strictly speaking, would be in Year 2 this academic year, wouldn't she? But given how much school she's missed, and her situation, of course – she will obviously have priority – they are happy to slot her into a Year 1 class. Oh, by the way, has she been getting work through from their online thingy okay? Only they said they would give her some log-in details to get onto their virtual learning thingy. I forgot to ask the other day. Did they?'

Christine was about as tech-savvy as I was, so luckily, I understood what she meant by 'online thingy'. 'They have,' I confirmed. And Mike got her all set up. 'I imagined she would be joining a virtual class or something, with other kids, but it's not like that, it's just like a replica of the lessons, adapted for her, to be done in her own time, but she's been doing very well with it.'

'Ah, that's brilliant. I do love it when a plan comes together. Anyway, does eleven tomorrow morning work for you? It's with the head teacher, Mr Patterson. Only I promised I'd call his secretary back to confirm asap.'

'Hmm,' I said, 'I'm not sure. I'll need to go and check my schedule …'

'Oh, right,' she said. Then half a second later, the penny dropped. 'Doh,' she said. 'I'm being slow on the uptake, aren't I?'

I laughed. 'I wish I did have a flipping schedule. Most of the time I don't even know what *day* it is. Oh, for something in the diary. *Anything* in the diary. Though I'm excited to be able to plan some garden fun at last. And for someone to actually use Mike's hot-tub installation. It feels like a grand exhibition space with zero visitors. Not that I can really see Mum and Dad clambering into it anytime soon …'

We chatted amiably for a few minutes about nothing very much. Unlike me, Christine did have a pretty busy schedule, trying to fire-fight so many lockdown-related crises. 'Can *I* book an hour in your hot tub some time?' she asked. 'Pretty please?'

'Absolutely any time,' I said. 'Since you're officially allowed, we could even have our next meeting in it,'

I suggested. 'Handily, it's big enough for us to socially distance.'

'Oh, how wonderful would *that* be? You're on. Oh, and one more thing: I emailed you Amelie's aunt's number half an hour or so ago. I was thinking you might like to introduce yourself to her ahead of us fixing up the face-to-face with Amelie. You're the one best placed to answer her questions, after all. And charm her, of course ... I did sense she's proceeding with caution. Though that's absolutely as it should be, of course. Are you happy to make contact? At your convenience, of course. I obviously wasn't – ahem – going to give her your number.'

'Of course I am,' I said, my investigative antennae immediately twitching.

Because she was probably best placed to answer some of my questions as well.

Ten minutes later, and having set my phone to No Caller ID, I made the call. 'I'm just ringing for a chat really, Robyn,' I started, after we'd exchanged the usual niceties about the lockdown, 'and to see if there's anything you wanted to ask me about Amelie.'

The woman had sounded a little nervous when I'd introduced myself, and, I thought I detected, also wary. Which was fair enough. I knew little about her, but I suspected she was processing a great deal. Not just about her newly rediscovered sister, and the fact that she had nearly killed both herself and her daughter, but about the whole business of finding herself embroiled in the complex machinery of social services – dealing with all the different departments and agencies, the faceless public servants, all the care and legal jargon. The world I worked in, so familiar to me and my colleagues, was, for most people, a whole other one; a landscape that was completely unfamiliar. I imagined she must, at the heart of it, be stupefied that the little niece she'd lost touch with was now legally a part of that world.

'I still haven't entirely made my mind up yet about how much I can help,' she said carefully, almost as if having been instructed to do so. Perhaps she'd taken legal advice. Again, fair enough. 'But I have been speaking with the social worker, and I was sent a copy of her care plan to fill in any gaps.'

'That's great,' I said brightly. 'That's obviously going to be so helpful in giving us the bigger picture.'

'So what sort of thing do they need?' she asked, turning questioner herself. 'There doesn't seem to be a lot on there. And they only have the one address for her, which I presume is the current one. Well, *was* the current one. No longer the current one, obviously. What do they want me to add?'

The care plan for a foster child contained all the salient information: parents' names, their address, dates of birth, etc., and then, if applicable, the name of the child's school. Plus, their allocated social worker (established or newly appointed), their GP, etc. and the details of the new foster carer, plus a write-up of what led to the child being in care. There would normally also be a section written by a social worker, telling new carers a bit about the child – their likes and dislikes, their personality, what they enjoyed doing at school and in leisure time, their daily routine, their bedtime routine and so on. In cases like this, however, where so little was known, there would obviously be a lot of gaps.

Robyn, having suggested she might want to be involved in Amelie's future, would, of course, be able to see it too. And would have been encouraged to add to it if she could, as it would form part of the paperwork when the case came to court. And it seemed she might have some things to add.

'Has Amelie spoken to you about living in Scotland?' she asked.

'Scotland? Not to me. Did they live in Scotland at some point then?'

'Yes, for a time, though in all sorts of places. It was impossible to keep track of them. Once her mental health took that really big dive, my sister never stayed anywhere for too long. I think you know about her … condition …' She checked herself. 'Sorry. Of course you do. If she had one of her episodes – thinking she was being followed, or her phone hacked or whatever – she'd just pack up and leave with Amelie at a moment's notice. She never did it properly – no removal vans or taking any furniture with them or anything. She'd leave everything bar a couple of bags of clothes and bits and so on, and then either hitch a ride or use whatever money she'd managed to stash away and hop on a train or a taxi to another area, then present themselves as homeless and start all over again.'

In contrast to her earlier reticence, Robyn now spoke quickly, the words tumbling out of her. 'Ah, well, if they lived in Scotland for a while, maybe that's why we know so little about Amelie's past,' I suggested. 'Completely different social services and healthcare, etc., that's if she was even legally registered with any of them.' I had a thought then. She'd said 'that' really big dive, as if there was a significant moment she knew all about. 'Did they live there long?' I asked.

'I don't know. She was in Scotland the last time I had any contact with her, so I assumed they must still be somewhere there. I was shocked to find she'd moved so far away, to be honest. And her popping up on social media like that was sheer fluke.'

'So you'd completely lost track of her? I'm assuming you didn't live nearby then?'

'No, I was down on the south coast of England, with my mum. And once we had the big bust-up after she lost the twins, she cut me off completely.'

So there it was. It wasn't wishful thinking on Amelie's part. The twins *had* actually existed. And perhaps what Robyn had just told me explained why there was nothing on Kelly's file. Well, not that we'd been told about anyway.

'Oh, my goodness,' I said. 'Amelie's spoken about the twins. I wasn't sure if it was something' – I chose my words carefully – 'that had been put into her head during one of mum's mental health crises.'

'Oh, they were very much real,' she said. 'Well, in utero, in any rate.' She sighed heavily. 'Everything became *so* much worse after she lost them.'

Robyn went on to describe a heartbreaking and all-too-familiar story. A one-night stand – Kelly could apparently be highly promiscuous during her manic phases – then the discovery of an unwanted pregnancy, and a twin one, to boot. And one which Robyn, highly concerned, urged her sister to terminate, for both financial reasons – she only worked sporadically, as far as Robyn knew – and because of her always-fragile mental state. 'There was also the worry about taking the meds she was on while pregnant. All in all, continuing with the pregnancy was the worst possible decision, but she was determined to, and all I could do was support her from a distance. But then she lost them,' Robyn continued. 'First one, then the other. I didn't have all the details – I was hearing everything second hand, of course – but I think placental insufficiency or some-thing. They thought they might be able to deliver the second one safely, but sadly not so …'

'Oh my God – how far long was she?'

'Twenty-three, twenty-four weeks or so? It was just awful. I left Mum – she was very ill with cancer by this time, so that was hard in itself – and went up to stay for a couple of days. She had some friend who was helping a bit with Amelie, but she was an awful person.

A neighbour. Weird woman. Definitely on drugs. The whole thing was just a huge mess ... and poor Amelie. It was all so bloody wretched.'

My head was still reeling from all the grim facts I was hearing. Mum very ill with cancer. The one-night stand. The doomed pregnancy. Amelie primed and ready for little siblings that never came. 'It sounds just awful,' I agreed.

'It was. And that was when her mental health really deteriorated. I suggested she and Amelie come back down south and live with me for a bit, and she just lost it. She began to go downhill very quickly,' Robyn said. 'Demanded that I leave and when I told her I was concerned about Amelie's welfare, accused me of trying to steal her. It was just *horrible*. I wanted to speak with her GP, but the receptionist wouldn't let me, and then I got scared about reporting her to social services or anyone, and Amelie being taken away from her as well. I just couldn't do that to her – to *them*. I just knew I had to get myself out of the situation, because I was just making her worse. I hoped she'd calm down if I went. And I was probably right to. As soon as I got home she started calling and accusing me of all sorts of things. She'd got it into her head that the babies hadn't died. They'd been stolen while she was under anaesthetic, by – don't laugh – the FBI, so they could use them for experiments or something. That was the last conversation we had. God knows what she filled Amelie's head with after that.'

*More of the same*, I thought. *Much, much more of the same*. Again, I was stunned that all this had happened under the radar, but perhaps Robyn's decision – and it wasn't for me to judge her in the making of it – had been key. 'So you never spoke again after that?'

'No, she blocked my number. Blocked me from all her social media. I then had a change of mind; Mum had died by this time, and I was able to get my head together. So I spoke to her GP surgery again, and was at least reassured that they said they'd do a welfare visit or something – I can't remember all the details. Anyway, I never heard back, and with Mum having gone and sorting out the funeral and everything, and with so much to sort out …' She paused. 'Anyway, when I next made it up there, a few weeks later, she'd gone.'

I was still full of questions but was just about to speak when we were interrupted by the familiar sound of a ringing doorbell, closely followed by a bark.

'Look, I have to go,' Robyn said. 'That'll be my friend with the other dogs. We walk a couple of our elderly neighbours' dogs with ours,' she qualified, 'because they're still shielding. It's been a nice lockdown routine, to be honest.' She chuckled slightly. 'Made me even think of getting another one …'

*Or perhaps a child to help you walk it?* I thought to myself. I crossed the fingers of my free hand without even thinking. 'It sounds it. And I imagine they are really grateful, too. Oh, and speaking of lockdown,' I said, 'before you go, I think you have a special dispensation to travel, given the circumstances. Re your coming to visit, that is. Did they tell you?'

'They did.' I heard the sound of a door opening, a muffled 'I'll be right there', another bark. 'D'you want to text me your availability over the next 10 days or so?' Robyn asked. 'I'll just need to find myself some key worker's accommodation or something. I'm not sure where we are with all the rule changes.'

I told her I would, then said goodbye and hung up, having made a mental note to make a real note of everything she'd told me, then did exactly that, sitting in the garden, at the patio table. There was so much more to ask, to know, to feel hopeful about now. I couldn't wait to meet her. I picked up my phone and typed a text.

*Any day from next Tuesday. Any day at all.*

# Chapter 16

The next day, as we were getting ready for the all-important school visit, I received a text message reply from Robyn. It was very positive, thanking me for our chat the day before, and best of all with three or four dates she could do the following week. She'd also organised somewhere to stay. Her good friend and neighbour had kindly offered to loan her a small campervan overnight, so she didn't need to worry about finding somewhere to stay. It had definitely been a worry. I was as confused as she'd been, but a little googling seemed to have confirmed that hotels and guest houses were still not open to the public, and that, despite the circumstances, most would probably have refused to take her; after all, there was still the option of the now ubiquitous Zoom, and it would have been hard to convince anyone of the vital importance of Amelie actually meeting her flesh-and-blood aunt face-to-face. She'd been living with conspiracy theories for too long.

I texted back and agreed a date which was just over a week away, but I decided not to tell Amelie about the visit yet. She'd only get overexcited and I was keen that it didn't interfere with her settling in at school. I did, however, want to do a little groundwork, gently probing to see if she had any memories of her aunt, which she presumably would, since she definitely had memories of the siblings that had never come home.

First things first, however. And, in this case, that meant prepping her for the school visit.

'So, best behaviour,' I said, as I tightened the bows in her pigtails, 'and let the headmaster see what a good girl you are, then you'll be able to go there and play with all the other children. Won't that be nice?'

She nodded, smiling at herself in my bedroom mirror, and tilting her head from side to side, as if practising in preparation for the big moment.

'Yes,' she said, 'and I will be the goodest girl, I promise. No baby talk. Just six talk.' The smile widened. 'I can't wait to see all my friends again!'

I turned to put the hairbrush back in my dressing-table drawer and frowned. Surely Amelie didn't think she was going to see her old school friends? No, I told myself, she probably meant the new children she would meet; she seemed to assume that everybody was already her best friend, didn't she? But I was to be quickly reacquainted with the reality that we'd been in lockdown since we'd had her, and that all kinds of things might be going on in her mind now that we were properly integrating with the wider world. Because as we approached the small primary school around the corner from our house, I realised that she *did* actually believe we had been headed for her old school.

As the school came into view, I felt her grip on my hand tighten, and a tug as she came to an abrupt stop. 'No!' she said, sounding horrified. 'This isn't my school! We can't go in that place. It's not safe!' She tugged on my hand harder then, to pull me back. 'Stop! Look, there's cameras, *spy* cameras. Can't you *see* them?'

I looked across the playground, to the school building and, yes, there were cameras. I bent down in front of Amelie and took her other hand as well. 'Look at me, sweetie,' I urged her. 'Don't look up there. Look at *me*, okay?'

She dragged her gaze back to me, and I could see genuine terror in her face. 'But they're *watching* us,' she whispered. 'We can't go in there.'

'Sweetheart, I promise you that this school is a safe place. Amelie, listen. I pinky promise you it's safe, do you hear? Those cameras are to keep all the *school children* safe, so that if anyone comes into the playground that isn't meant to be there, the teachers can see them straight away and they send someone out to them. Do you see? Just like it was in your last school, I imagine. Did they have cameras there?'

She glanced up and back. 'Yes, but Mummy hid me. Can you hide me? So the spies can't see me?'

I thought back to the conversation I'd had with Christine about her mum's bizarre behaviours at Amelie's former school and how it had been the head there who'd first raised concerns about them. 'Sweetie,' I replied gently, 'those cameras are there to *look after* you. To keep you safe. There is really nothing to be afraid of.'

Confusion clouded her face and, not for the first time, I felt a surge of anger. How had this child been left for so long to live with the consequences of a parent with a mental illness? Of course, I was now able to answer my own question in my head: because of all the moving around they had done. No schools or local authorities would have had the opportunity to get involved, because she'd obviously left the area before wheels could be set in motion.

'Are you sure?' Amelie asked, still looking anything but. I stood back up briskly, squeezed her hands and smiled down at her. 'I have never been surer about *anything*,' I reassured her. 'Do you really think I would *ever* bring you somewhere that I didn't think was completely safe? Of course I wouldn't. And you went to the supermarket with Mike yesterday, didn't you?'

She digested this. And nodded, seeming to find it reassuring, just as I'd hoped she would. And presumably had the previous day. There had not been a word about the supermarket cameras when they'd arrived home; just excitement about bunting and party plates and balloons. So perhaps the same would apply here.

I could only keep my fingers crossed. 'Come on then,' I said. 'Now we know just what a safe place this new school is, we can go in and visit with Mr Patterson. And we can even wave up at the camera on our way in, if you like, so the teachers will know we are good people too.'

Amelie began to walk again, though still keeping a tight grip on my hand. But stopped again, just as we were about to enter the building. 'Casey,' she whispered, 'my friends aren't going to be here, are they?'

It was spoken more as an acknowledgement – a sad acknowledgement – than a question. 'No, darling,' I said gently. 'You're right. I'm afraid your old friends won't be, because they don't go to this school. But there will be new friends. There are lots of girls and boys here, and I'm sure all of them can't *wait* to make friends with you.'

'Okay,' she said. And though her expression suggested she felt like a lamb being led to the slaughter, I counted that moment of clarity, of Amelie engaging with reality, as a win. Because the real world was much the safest place for her.

I was also really pleased with how the meeting went. I knew Mr Patterson had been briefed on Amelie's background and situation, but even had he not been, he struck me as the kind of teacher who could just 'read' a child and interact with them accordingly. To which Amelie responded very positively. It was only when he brought in her class teacher and one of the teaching

197

assistants that, perhaps slightly triggered by having an audience of three now, she had the odd lapse into switching to her baby voice. I needn't have worried though – her odd lisp, and expressions of babyish syntax, only prompted several 'Oh, isn't she adorable!' looks in my direction.

'Oh, and we can't wait to see them,' her teacher, a pretty twenty-something called Miss Stanforth, exclaimed delightedly, after Amelie had told them that she would go home and do them all a painting. 'You know, we are all *so* excited to have you come and join us, Amelie. And tell me, what's your favourite colour? So we can make some nice stickers for your tray and your coat peg.'

Amelie thought about this for a long moment. 'I like all the colours,' she opted for finally. 'But I like black the best.' Then, seeing the expressions this choice had provoked in all of us, she added, 'Black's safe. When it's black, no one can see you.'

'Oh, but we *do* want to see you,' Miss Stanforth answered, not skipping a beat. 'So what's your second-favourite colour?'

'Sparkly pink,' Amelie said immediately. 'Yes, definitely sparkly pink. I have a headband that colour so I'll wear that tomorrow, so you'll know it's me and your cameras will let me in.'

Two pairs of eyes swivelled in my direction, this time in some confusion. From Mr Patterson, however, I noticed, there was a discreet, understanding nod. He'd obviously been fully briefed on Amelie's history. 'We were looking at the security cameras on our way in,' I explained to the two teachers. 'Amelie always likes to check them out, don't you, sweetie?'

'And do they meet with your approval, Amelie?' Mr Patterson asked, a hint of a smile playing across his features.

'Yes,' she answered, nodding. 'Because I know they're all safe now.'

'And you'll be safe *here*,' he replied. I could have hugged him.

There was a spring in Amelie's step as we headed back home. 'Can we go back in the morning?' she asked. 'I want to meet my new friends.'

'Not tomorrow,' I told her. 'You're going to start there next week, so we have time to get some uniform and the other things you'll need. A new backpack, and a lunch box, and –'

'But I already have a lunch box. At home.' My antennae crackled. It was the first time, I realised, since telling me about the twins' teddies, that Amelie had mentioned any of her old possessions. And the first time she'd ever mentioned her old home, come to think of it, without any prompting from me. 'The one with dinosaurs on,' she finished. 'I want that one. Can we go and get it?'

I wasn't sure how to answer that, so held off replying for a moment, taking refuge in us looking right, left and right again as we crossed the road into our street. 'I'm afraid not, sweetie,' I eventually plumped for, 'but I'm sure we'll be able to find another one with dinosaurs on it. Any dinosaurs in particular?'

'*All* the dinosaurs,' she answered. 'T-Rexes and Diplodocuses and Stegosauruses and Triceratops …' And I had an image of her, a very poignant one, with her mum, carefully reciting all the names as she pointed to them. 'Is it burned?' she said suddenly, once her list came to an end.

'It probably is, I'm afraid, sweetie,' I said. 'But as I say, there will be others, and –'

''s'okay,' she said, shrugging. 'I don't mind a new one. And a bottle for my squash?'

'And a bottle for your squash.'

Which seemed to satisfy her, because she then switched to smelling all our neighbours' flowers, but she was clearly still thinking hard about everything because just as we were approaching our house she stopped on the pavement. 'Shall I tell my new friends you're my second mummy now?'

I was now looking for my keys in my bag so, again, fumbled around to give myself time. I always hated it when younger foster children said things like this, because it was hard, sometimes heartbreaking, to have to explain to confused little ones that we weren't their real family, just foster parents for however long we needed to be that. We were, and are, supposed to be led by the child, but if a child called me 'Mummy', say, we were always encouraged to steer them gently away from that line of thinking. To remind them that they had a mummy, always (assuming they were alive), even if they didn't live with them. It was tricky with very young children, however, as they often said 'Mummy' automatically, and then simply failed to correct themselves. In cases like that, however, I could never be so direct with a child, so I'd just go along with it, essentially by saying nothing, and hope it would sort itself out eventually.

The whole issue of 'family' was often a minefield. Over the years I'd come to understand that one of the first things a new foster child did was work out where they fitted into ours. They would be introduced to the wider family, meet grandchildren, cousins, temporary siblings and so on, and would often try to work out where they came in their perceived pecking order. They lived with us, so were they 'higher' than grandchildren who came to visit? Or did the blood tie between us make them 'lower'? A difficult thing to navigate – who would ever want to assess their level of importance in an organic structure like a family? – but for a displaced child, especially one who had no idea whether this would be a long-term arrangement, or who had no idea if they would ever have their own family to return to, it was a completely understandable survival strategy. A normal human instinct, in fact, for helping them begin to feel secure again.

The peculiarity of lockdown meant Amelie had less of that to deal with than most, since, for most of the time, it was just her, me and Mike. It was perhaps natural, therefore, for her to have reached the conclusion that we were, indeed, her new mummy and daddy, so I was heartened that she'd instead used the word 'second', as it made it easier to introduce the idea that I was a slightly different figure in her life. 'Well, Amelie,' I replied, 'you know, you're very lucky. You are right. You do kind of have two families. You have Mike and me, who are kind of like your aunty and uncle, then you have your mummy, who you speak with, but don't live with right now. And also,' I added, this seeming like as good a time as any, 'I don't know if you remember her, but you also have a lovely aunty called Robyn, don't you? Your mummy's sister. Do you remember her?'

Once again, Amelie screwed up her face in thought. 'I think I sort of do,' she said. 'Is she the lady who bought me the baby doll and all the dolly clothes?'

'She might have been,' I said. 'Do you remember when that was?'

'In the flat in the brown building, I think,' she said, after a moment. 'I think Mummy said she was. Robyn after robins. Like the bird,' she added helpfully. 'Because robins come at Christmas.'

I slipped the key into the lock and opened the front door. 'They do indeed,' I said. 'And perhaps it's because your Aunty Robyn was born at Christmas?'

Amelie looked up at me as she pulled off her cardigan. 'I think she was,' she said. 'Do you know her?'

'I don't know her, not yet, but I have spoken to her,' I said. 'In fact, she's coming down soon for a visit. To see you.'

'Me?'

'Yes, *of course* you,' I said, grinning and pulling gently on her pigtails. 'She wants to see how you're getting on.'

'Oh,' she said, shrugging. 'Okay. Now can we go on your tablet and look at dinosaur lunchboxes?'

'We can indeed,' I said. 'Then we'd better start getting organised for our barbecue tomorrow, hadn't we?'

She clapped her hands together. 'I had forgotted about that! Are we going to make the bunting?'

'We are going to make the bunting. And a cake, too. It's a party so we *have* to have cake, don't we?'

'With sprinkles! We bought sprinkles in the shops yesterday specially!'

So on the subject of Aunty Robyn, that clearly was that. At least for now, and that was just fine by me. I was just happy that the mention of her name hadn't fazed Amelie. Yes, it was still a very long way from that to the loving, lasting relationship that I knew could, if everything worked out, have the potential to totally transform Amelie's life, but at least it was a start. At least I hadn't scared the horses.

For now, though, I was happy to live entirely in the moment and focus on the loving relationships in my own universe. And, in tune with the sunshine, already streaming across the kitchen floor when I came down the following morning, my heart could not have been fuller. I was going to be able to hug my mum and dad for the first time in *months*. Well, once we'd all done our Covid tests, obviously.

In the meantime, a busy morning beckoned. We'd promised Amelie a sprinkle-doused cake and balloons in the garden so while she attended to the former – and with free rein with the contents of my cake-decorating box – I spent an exhausting hour blowing up some 30-odd balloons, and tying them to lengths of ribbon, ready to hang outside, before tackling the usual business of preparing everything that didn't come under the umbrella of 'things that go on the actual barbecue' (i.e. most of it) and ticking them off the 'party jobs' list Amelie had written up the night before, being, as ever, in her element as a party planner.

Mike, of course, was conspicuous by his absence. Once he'd taken the cover off the hot tub so Amelie could have a splash about in it once she'd finished all her jobs, he'd gone into full-on barbecue man mode and disappeared into his shed, emerging a little later with the barbecue itself plus all the special bits of equipment he liked to keep safely wrapped up in there.

Then it was simply a question of digging out his special barbecuing apron and fully inhabiting his role. Like many other women, I never ceased to be amazed at the transformation of men into gourmet Michelin-starred chefs whenever the word 'barbecue' was mentioned. Not that I ever complained; I could think of little I'd enjoy less than standing in front of a pile of hot, smoking, spitting coals, grilling lumps of meat.

And it made him happy – even the fact that his tools were so shiny and clean because he'd taken the time to clean, polish and dry them all properly before he'd put them to bed the previous autumn.

'And to *wrap them up* properly,' he added, having brought them all in so we could marvel at his array of pristine tongs and griddles and skewers. 'That's what some people forget. You need to wrap them up properly to keep the damp out.'

'They look *amazing*,' I intoned, trying but not quite managing to keep the sarcasm out of my voice as I toiled away, prepping four different salads and rummaging in the cupboards for all the necessary condiments, plus the ingredients to make 'his' special barbecue sauce recipe. 'But it's getting on for noon and I still have a lot to do, and you need to go and pick up Mum and Dad in 20 minutes, so –'

'*Chill*, Case,' he drawled, patting me helpfully on the shoulder. 'Honestly. It's just a small barbecue, not a banquet. And remember – *I'm* going to be the one doing all the cooking, so you will be able to relax. Great cake decorating, Amelie, by the way,' he added, 'assuming there *is* a cake buried underneath all that stuff somewhere. Anyway, I shall look forward to – ouch! Enough with the ruddy tea towel, woman! *Ouch!*'

Ah, this was more like it. Happy days.

An hour later, once my sister and my parents had arrived, I was able to have my first proper chance to see Amelie interacting within a proper family dynamic;

incredible in itself, when you thought about it. Yes, she'd experienced having other little ones to stay for respite, and, of course, Katie, but this was the first time she'd been around people in our family in the flesh, and our familiarity around each other made her initially a little shy; as she watched Donna and my mum and dad come out into the garden, she remained in the hot tub, clearly happy to be observer rather than participant for a while.

I didn't push it; despite her obvious excitement about having new 'friends' coming to play, there must be all kinds of things going through Amelie's head, I suspected, and probably anxieties around whether all these people were 'safe'. From what little she'd disclosed, and from the things her Aunt Robyn had told me, I imagined she'd little experience of family members popping round, let alone coming over for parties. Only a small one, in this case, but still no doubt a bit intimidating. Yes, she'd 'met' Mum and Dad through the screen of my laptop, but that was quite different from actually seeing them in the flesh. Was she worried about bugs? That they might be spies? That they might wish her harm? Her assessing gaze, from across the garden, seemed to suggest so, the way she held the big plastic water-soaker-blaster thing Mike had treated her to in the supermarket so that, should she need to, she could repel them as well.

Happily, Mum and Dad – and Donna, come to that – were well used to interacting with the kids we looked after, having been on the fostering sidelines over quite a few years now, as troubled, and often challenging, children came and went. They were happy, therefore, to give her the space she needed for a bit, simply waving and shouting hellos, and waiting for my cue before coaxing her to join us.

Once I *had* coaxed her out, though, Amelie was soon keen to interact, wrapping herself in a towel and hugging everyone with gusto. She had never mentioned any grandparents, or Robyn, only her mother, who I assumed must have played very little part in her daughter's life, so it was interesting to see how she made a particular beeline for my dad.

'Are you my grandad now?' she asked him, and pretty matter-of-factly, having climbed up onto the garden chair next to his. 'Because I don't have a grandad, because my mummy said he died.'

Dad smiled. 'You can call me grandad if you want to,' he said. 'And that lady there' – he smiled at Mum – 'you can call Nanna if you like. We're happy to be your stand-in grandparents for as long as you need us. Now, how about you show me what you can do with that scary-looking thing?' he added, pointing towards the oversized water pistol that was now on the grass beneath her. 'Only one thing – no squirting it at me, okay? Aunty Donna, on the other hand …' He winked at me and my sister.

'Cheers, Dad,' mouthed Donna, rolling her eyes. But I could see she was happy enough to take one for the team.

Which was good, because Amelie didn't need telling twice. Ice broken, and ice-cold water soon aimed at my poor sister, the party was at last under way.

And what an edifying afternoon it was. Though the absence of my kids was always going to be difficult, my gratitude at being able to see at least some of my family was immense. Which made it feel all the more poignant that in the midst of it all was a little girl for whom life was very different. We'd been parted temporarily from those we loved most, and that was hard, but for her there was almost no one to reconnect with. Her mum had gone and it looked like she was never coming back to her, she had no grandad or grandma, and her aunt was a woman she only dimly remembered, for bringing her a doll and some doll's clothes.

Or so I'd thought. Later on, when I was tucking her into bed, she talked happily of her 'second family', and when we would next have them over, and I thought I'd take the opportunity to steer the conversation round to the brief one we'd had the previous day.

'And your Aunty Robyn is coming soon to visit, too,' I reminded her. 'She can't wait to see you. Won't that be exciting?'

A frown of anxiety crossed her pretty features. 'Will she bring presents?' she asked.

'I don't know,' I answered truthfully, for I had no idea if she would, then, to head off any subsequent disappointment, added, 'She might decide to wait till she knows what you'd like.'

Amelie nodded sleepily. 'I like *all* the toys,' she said finally. 'But I don't have to go away with her, do I?'

Could she have read my mind? I was just trying to come up with an answer, to reassure her that, for now at least, she wasn't going anywhere, when she grabbed my hand. 'Because I want to stay *here* now.'

'I know, sweetie,' I said, my brain whirring madly. It was one thing to worry about Robyn not wanting to take on Amelie. Quite another to contemplate the possibility that to have to leave us might distress Amelie greatly. Yet it was obviously completely logical that it might. This child who appeared to have little attachment to her mother was becoming attached to me and Mike – and why ever would she not? We were perhaps the only *really* safe place she had ever known.

I leaned forward and kissed her forehead. 'I know,' I said again. And, to my *very* profound relief, her eyes closed.

# Chapter 17

The next day I received a call to say that I could take Amelie to the local school for either three full days or five half days, starting the following Monday. I decided to opt for the five half days as, after being such a long time at home, I figured full days might be too much for her at first. I also liked the fact that we could establish a new routine, to get her into the rhythm of a normal week, since normal weeks finally looked like becoming re-established sooner rather than later.

I was also happy to do that for myself. I was naturally a lark, and having Amelie in school every morning would allow me to get on with all sorts of jobs, plus perhaps amble round the park with Riley and our daughter-in-law Lauren and some of the grandkids, even if we had to do it in rotation.

What Amelie had said to me on the night of the barbecue was much on my mind. She had not mentioned it again, and I had not brought the subject up. Though when I'd logged it in my record, I'd made both actual and mental notes that when the psychologist got back in touch with a date to have a session with Amelie, it was something that I hoped she'd probe instead. Though there was no rush. (Which was good, because the waiting list was immense.) Discussion of Amelie's thoughts about moving on from us were, for the moment, still academic anyway. Should things go well with her aunt, there would obviously be discussions with her about the best way forward, and if they didn't, we would still be on the original trajectory: of Kelly legally relinquishing care of her daughter, and a plan for Amelie's eventual adoption.

I was less concerned about the latter plan now than I had been. In fact, over the past two or three weeks, I had worried less generally, as, day by day, I could see Amelie changing. Yes, she still had her little foibles, but they were becoming less pronounced and I could see her begin to question all the 'truths' she had previously lived by. Though her concern about spy cameras was still very present, she no longer worried about bugs round the house, and ate, by and large, completely normally. All sound evidence of the adaptability of children placed in new surroundings, which never ceased to amaze me.

In the here and now, however, Amelie was totally focussed on school, and being as prepared for her new adventure as she could be. Her new school stuff, carefully chosen and delivered a few days later, was checked over and set out over and over again. And she was a little piqued that, for the moment, my having decided on the five mornings option, she would have no use for her new dinosaur lunchbox, and was only mollified when I explained that we could still have a packed lunch, only in the garden, or perhaps the park, once I'd collected her.

'But I still need my backpack,' she said, on the Sunday evening, before her first day. 'And all my pens and my notebook, so I can write down all the naughty children's names.'

I almost laughed out loud at this – I had expected her to say spellings – and I could see Mike was tickled as well.

'Woah, slow down, kiddo,' he said. 'I really don't think you will need to be writing down any naughty children's names. That's the teacher's job. And besides, I doubt they'll *be* any naughty children. I'm quite sure they'll all be good boys and girls, just like you, okay?'

Amelie considered this. 'But there might be. Shall I just tell the teacher?'

She looked up at him with innocent and genuinely enquiring eyes. I had no idea where she'd got the impression that it was her job to be class informant, but it was probably all bound up within the mish-mash of oddities in her brain. And after all, if you live in a world full of perceived spies, wasn't it logical that you should engage in some spying too?

But it was just another thing she had to be gently disabused of.

'Well, yes, you *could*,' Mike suggested gently. 'But you know what I think? That the main thing is not to worry *too* much about what anyone else is getting up to. Just you concentrate on what you're doing, and being a good girl for the teachers, okay?'

It was spot on. Just a gentle nudge. She would doubtless soon find her feet. We simply didn't know what other outrageous things her mum had put into her head during her periods of sickness, and I was reassured that Mr Patterson knew the background anyway. More pressing was knowing how to dissuade her from stuffing 26 of her drawings into her bag, ready to be handed out to anyone deserving who came into her orbit.

'I'm not sure you need to take that many, Amelie,' I said.

'But I need them for all my new friends and teachers,' she explained.

'But, lovey, I don't think there are that many people in your class, at least not right now. Perhaps leave some at home? You can always take more later.'

'But some people,' she persisted, with her usual logic, 'might want *two*.'

'Well, if they tell you they do,' I said, 'you can always bring them another, can't you?'

'But I *want* to take them all,' she said, pouting at me crossly.

'But you *can't*, kiddo,' Mike said, his tone making clear the discussion was over. 'You need room in your bag for all the things you'll be bringing back with you. Your reading books and homework, for instance.'

This proved sufficient distraction – a new reading book! – and I was glad of it. It was such a big thing for any child to start in a new school, and I really didn't want it marred by the other kids finding her odd, or ingratiating, and perhaps shunning her. She'd had such a patchy school experience, and had probably been deemed an oddball there, and I really wanted this new start to be a completely clean slate. I just hoped it would live up to her expectations.

Meanwhile, come Monday morning, my own expectations were exceeded. Having dashed off without breakfast, in the rush to get Amelie fed, dressed and ready, I was delighted to return home to the smell of bacon cooking.

'Sit yourself down in the garden,' Mike commanded, 'there are some pastries and juice at the table, and I'll be out with your full English breakfast in two minutes.'

Wow! Maybe I had been too quick to judge when it came to my husband cooking. All these years together now and this really was a first. Apart from barbecues, obviously, I had always been head cook in our house.

'Big mistake this, Mike,' I said, as we sat down to enjoy our al fresco breakfast. 'I'm going to expect this more often now. What are we celebrating, anyway?'

'Having a couple of hours to ourselves?' he suggested. 'It's been a while, hasn't it?'

I gaped at him. 'Love, I think we've spent more time

in each other's company these past few months than we have in our entire *marriage*. It's a miracle we haven't killed each other, to be honest.'

'We've not done bad, have we?' he said, as he cut a piece of bacon. 'We've rubbed along alright. Though this bloody lockdown is driving me insane now. You know, I was looking out on the garden while I was emptying the dishwasher and I was seriously considering building a treehouse. It was only the fact that I realised we didn't have a tree big enough that stopped me. It's so boring having absolutely nothing to do. Can you believe I was even watching a YouTube video about how to make your own bread?'

I could. I had, only the previous evening, seriously started considering the purchase of a second-hand sewing machine. How hard could it be to make your own clothes, after all? Which was patently ridiculous. I hated sewing. And with my middle-aged eyesight, I could hardly even thread a bloody needle in any case. 'Deep breaths,' I said, 'and the feeling will pass. And it can't be long now, surely, before they allow you back to work? And make the most of the peace,' I said. 'I was just thinking on the walk home. It's about time for us to do another respite …'

With Mike's mind duly concentrated, and his carpentry enthusiasms on hold for the time being, I then went back inside to call Amelie's social worker, Andy Clarke, having had a text from Robyn to confirm a date for her visit.

About which he already knew, since Robyn had obviously kept him in the loop. 'Oh, I'm glad you've rung,' he said as soon as he picked up. 'In fact, I was about to call you, to check the date worked for you. And to see where we are with Amelie before I come out. Have you made any further inroads into how she feels about it all?'

I had already written up the few memories Amelie had told me she had about her aunt and had also added to my log what she'd said about not wanting to be taken away by her. 'Have you any thoughts on how I should handle that?' I asked. 'I just didn't know how to respond,' I said, 'and I really still don't. And I was wondering – Robyn was frank with me about Kelly's conviction that she was trying to steal Amelie from her. I wonder if Amelie had been privy to any conversations that might have taken place. What she said to me does suggest that she might have.'

'Well, I've spoken to the aunt at length as well,' he said. 'And what I suspect is more likely is that it's all come from Mum, in much the same way as she'd become convinced that her twins had been stolen from her; all part of the bigger picture that the world was out to get her. I wouldn't dwell on it all right now, though, since it's all hypothetical. And in any case, if it does look as if her aunt is going to play a part going forward, it'll be a fairly slow process. So I suggest sticking to the line that she's not going anywhere right now is your best bet. I also think I should hold off coming out to see her myself, since I think it'll only confuse her. Let's wait till she and her aunt have met, and what the feedback from that is. It would be great to think they'll hit it off and a bond will be re-established, but that's by no means a given, is it? They might recoil from one another on sight, but if you gently lay some groundwork, I'm sure that'll help. By the way, a bit of info: Robyn's a nurse. And it occurred to me, as I was skimming through the notes earlier, that that might be a plus, given that Amelie sees hospitals as quote-unquote safe. Might be helpful to introduce that? Anyway, just a thought. It might reassure her.'

*Or not*, I thought, as I ended the call. In reality, I had no idea. I couldn't call it. I could only watch and wait and cross my fingers.

# Chapter 18

The day of Robyn's visit, at the end of that week, began, annoyingly, with rain. And though the prime minister had said the country's 'hibernation' was now coming to an end, Robyn was still not allowed in our house. While Amelie was in school, therefore, and Robyn was travelling to us in her campervan, Mike had gone round to our son Kieron's and borrowed the gazebo they used when putting on socials for their football team. Once erected in the garden, it lent an air of celebration. I could only hope it would prove to be auspicious.

Amelie's first week of school every morning had gone better than either Mike or I expected. I had been so used to getting calls from schools about children we were fostering ('Will you please come and fetch him ...', 'I'm afraid there has been an incident ...', 'We need to speak about her behaviour ...') that to hear nothing from this one, to hear nothing at *all*, was really quite something. As for Amelie herself, there was nothing in her demeanour to suggest that she was doing anything other than enjoying herself, adapting well to her completely new environment, as always, and chattering animatedly about it all the way home.

Today, however, primed as she had been that morning, her mind was on the upcoming visit.

'Did you tell the lady about presents?' she wanted to know, as we headed home, hoods up, to evade the worst of the still-falling drizzle. 'Do you think she'll bring another dolly?'

'I don't know, sweetie,' I said to her, 'remember? She might. She might not. We'll just have to wait and see, won't we? I know she's come a long way, though, and she might not have had time to get anything for you. Do you remember I told you she might prefer to ask you what you'd like? And she probably,' I added, this seeming a good time to introduce it, 'will have been very hard at work. Your aunty is a nurse, you see, and all the doctors, and nurses, and hospitals in the country have been very, very busy.'

'Does she wear a nurse's uniform?'

'I imagine she does, yes.'

'Shall I wear my nurse's uniform, so we match?'

Amelie loved my dressing-up box and though she didn't often play dress-up, she did alternate being a teacher and playing schools with all her soft toys, with playing hospitals, winding swathes of old rags round their various limbs and performing life-saving operations on her charges.

'I don't think she'll have her uniform on today, sweetie,' I told her. 'But I'm sure she'll be able to tell you all about it.'

'I want to be a nurse when I grow up. A nurse for sick children and babies. Does the lady live at the hospital like Mummy does?' she asked.

'No, she just works there. At least I think so,' I qualified. 'I'm not sure yet what kind of nurse she is. She might work at the local doctor's, or go into people's homes to help them. There are all different kinds of nurses, just like there are with doctors –'

Amelie tugged on my arm. 'But she might work at Mummy's hospital?'

'No, she doesn't work there. She lives quite a long way away. She –'

'And does she know about the bad mens?'

I stopped on the pavement, conscious that I should really seize this moment. 'You know what?' I said. 'Do you remember how we talked before you went to the supermarket with Mike?' She nodded. 'And do you remember what I told you about the FBI?'

She thought for a second. 'That they live in Merica.'

'America. That's right. They are a special police force, in another country called America, and it's actually *their job* to find bad men. Bad men, bad people, who live in America. So they don't spy on you, or watch you, or want to do you *any* harm. Mummy only thought that because she was sick and got confused. And your Aunty Robyn *knows* Mummy has been sick and been confused. Like me, and Mike, *and* you, she knows that there aren't really any bad mens who want to hurt us. And *that's* a pinky promise,' I finished, holding up my little finger.

Nodding solemnly, Amelie linked hers in mine. 'There,' I said. 'Done. Now we'd better get home before we're soaked through, hadn't we?'

'We did a song about rain today. Shall I sing it to you?' she asked. So we were done.

I pulled her hood further forward. 'Oh, absolutely.'

Because Robyn had sent a voice message with her ETA when she was 10 minutes distant, we were able to look out for her, and be ready to greet her. We'd also been organised in another key way, agreeing that once niece and aunt had spent sufficient time together, Mike, who would hover, awaiting my cue, would take Amelie off to the park, where he'd planned to meet up with Riley and Marley Mae, something I'd already told Amelie about. This would allow Robyn and I to also have some time together. I was sure she must have plenty she wanted to ask me.

'Ah, that must be her campervan,' I told Amelie as we watched it pull up.

'What's a campervan?' she asked.

I laughed. 'That is.'

'But that's a car,' she said.

'Not quite. It's a car with a bed in. And probably a little cooker, and some cupboards for plates and cups. So you can camp in it. That's why it's called a campervan.'

'Like a little house on wheels?'

'Like a little house on wheels.'

'To go on holidays?'

'Yes, people do that all the time.'

'Like Peppa Pig! I just membered! Peppa Pig has a campervan and they go on holiday in it! It has everything little. And a cosy cosy bed! Oh, I'd love to sleep in a campervan!'

'Me too,' I agreed. 'Really cosy.'

'So is the lady going to sleep in it?'

'Yes, tonight, I think. She's borrowed it specially.'

'Out there in the road?'

'No, I think she's going to go to a campsite. Anyway, shall we go and say hello?'

'Do you think she'll let me see inside?'

'Oh, I'm sure she will, sweetie, but let's think about that later. Look, she's getting out. Let's go and open the front door, shall we?'

Amelie poked me. 'And look! She has *presents*!'

We headed out to the hall and I crossed my fingers that the three packages Robyn held were indeed the much-anticipated presents. And when I opened the door, the wrapping paper – woodland animals – seemed to suggest I was right. Whatever the rights or wrongs of gentle bribery, I mentally gave her a high-five.

I also formed a very positive first impression. Not because I could learn much about her from studying her as she approached – a Breton-style T-shirt, jeans and trainers, a big messenger bag – but because she looked so much like her niece. The same big blue eyes, the same softly curling strawberry blonde hair, the same delicate nose and heart-shaped face. In fact, she looked more like Amelie than did her own mother. So much so, in fact, that I had a sudden mad eureka moment. Perhaps she *was* in fact her mother, and this was about to be some big showbiz reveal.

She also had a mask dangling from her wrist. 'Shall I –?' she began, obviously spotting that I didn't.

'I'm fine if you are,' I said. 'We'll just keep the required distance. Anyway, this is Amelie.'

'Oh, *Amelie*,' she said, 'it is *so* good to see you. And look at you! Goodness me, you are *such* a big girl now!' With kids, in my experience, some things never change: Amelie puffed up with delight. And I mentally high-fived her estranged aunty for a second time.

'Come on in out of the rain,' I said. 'And, er, straight out again. We've got a cover-up in the garden. This way. Unless you'd like to use the loo? I've disinfected everything.'

'That would be much appreciated,' she said. 'Would you mind –' she held the packages out, extending her arms fully, in that way we'd all come to consider normal. 'Unless you'd like to, Amelie?' She smiled at her niece, the warmth in her eyes unmistakeable. 'They're all for you, after all, as I suspect you might already have guessed. They're a little heavy though, so perhaps –'

'I'll take them,' I said, doing the same stiff-armed manoeuvre to take them from her. 'I wouldn't want you to drop them. Let's take them outside, shall we, sweetie, while your Aunty Robyn spends a penny? Straight on out back,' I added, nodding in the direction of the garden. 'Tea or coffee, or a cold drink?'

'Tea, please,' Robyn answered as she dived into the downstairs cloakroom. *Well*, I thought, *I suppose nobody's perfect*.

With Amelie hot on my heels and now 100 per cent focussed on the half-expected bumper bounty, I took the gifts out to the gazebo, and put them on the table, then went back inside to put the kettle on.

'I'll deal with that,' Mike said, having followed me in from the shed, so he could say hello.

'Did you *see*?' Amelie said, pointing excitedly back towards the garden. 'That lady brought me *three* presents!'

'Well, it's your lucky day then, kiddo,' he said. 'Three presents at once? I can't remember the last time I got three presents at once.'

'I don't mind sharing,' she said immediately. Which made my heart melt. And I was already struggling enough with my emotions as it was, it having hit me that while for Amelie this was, to all intents and purposes, just 'that lady', someone she'd only been told she had a connection to, for Robyn herself this was a very big deal. She didn't just know, she could feel, she could *see*, that this little girl was her flesh and blood, and

224

the rift with her sister, and accompanying loss of her, must have been very painful.

At least I hoped so, and nothing in the next 20 minutes or so led me to feel any differently. Tea and coffee and a glass of squash made, and delivered to the garden along with biscuits, Mike retired back inside and I kept a bit of distance. Not just physically, as required of Her Majesty's Government, but because I wanted to give them a decent amount of space so that Robyn didn't feel she was being scrutinised.

And the opening of all the gifts was, of course, *the* perfect gift, allowing them to focus on that, rather than the awkwardness of being so long estranged. And there was really no agenda, but them getting re-acquainted. For Amelie it was just time spent with a present-bearing and friendly lady, and for Robyn a chance to see what everyone else saw. A sweet, polite, beguiling little girl. And Amelie really was that; the eccentricities that had been so obvious when she'd come to us back in April were barely noticeable today.

There was much whooping and hand-clapping as the gifts were opened, one by one. There was a kit to paint and build a stained-glass butterfly mobile, a light-up electronic dance mat she could throw some serious shapes on and, best of all, judging by Amelie's shrieks of delight, a big box of Lego Super Mario Princess Peach, which I knew must have cost a small fortune.

Like any six-year-old, Amelie was keen to open everything, all at once, so at that point I did step in, and place an embargo on the Lego, instead suggesting that if she opened anything it ought to be the mobile kit, as it was something they could make a start on together. 'And I'll make more tea,' I suggested, as Robyn, smiling knowingly, started gathering up the mass of torn paper to make space for them to get everything out. I already knew Robyn had no children of her own, but if I hadn't known that I would have guessed otherwise. She seemed very maternal. Perhaps she worked in paediatrics?

'How's it going?' asked Mike, once I'd gone back inside.

'So far so good,' I said. 'They seem to be getting on well. No awkward silences. No awkward questions. I think Amelie is just seeing it as a visit from someone nice, who's bought her presents. And if that's what today amounts to, that's a positive enough start.'

And it continued in the same vein for the next hour. Not wanting to direct anything about this first encounter, I took the word 'supervised' with a very loose approach. In fact, while the two of them together painted two of the 'stained-glass' butterflies, I pottered around the garden, picking tomatoes and dead-heading flowers. The bits of conversation I picked up were innocuous and pleasant – Amelie telling Robyn about her new school friends and about life with me and Mike, and Robyn chipping in with little snippets about the work she did (she *was* a nurse in orthopaedics, it turned out) and her dog, a Dalmation called Rufus.

It was me who decided to bring things to a close, since the day was running out, and I knew Robyn still had to drive to the place she was staying at overnight, and I was still keen that we had some time to ourselves first.

'Now then, sweetie,' I said to Amelie, once I'd been shown the results of their combined labours, 'I think it's time to clear up and head down to the park. Marley-Mae and Riley are going to come down and meet you and Mike there, remember? While Aunty Robyn and I have a cup of tea and a chat before she leaves.'

For Amelie, who was close in age to my granddaughter and had already spoken to her several times via FaceTime, this proved as attractive a prospect as we had hoped. 'D'you want to come with us?' she asked Robyn. 'You can if you want to.' But when Robyn demurred, saying she'd love to but she was tired after her long journey, Amelie made no move to persuade her. Like any six-year-old, she was on to the next exciting thing, and while Mike went to fetch her wellies and raincoat, their goodbyes were light-hearted and low-key. (Plus, handily, she seemed to have forgotten about the campervan tour.)

Which was, I decided, exactly what was wanted. No big fuss; just a pleasant encounter between them, the promising start I had hoped for, with no heavy emotional moments.

So I really didn't see what happened next coming.

While I made another cup of tea (Amelie's aunt, it seemed, could drink tea like I drank coffee), Robyn, after carefully putting all the mobile kit bits away, took herself off for a second time to the loo. That she had been a while didn't particularly concern me, but when she eventually returned to the garden, I was surprised to see her clutching a wodge of tissue, and looking as though she'd been crying.

'Are you okay?' I said, as she sat down heavily on the chair across the table from me.

'Yes, I'm fine,' she said. 'It's all been just … well … a bit emotional today, that's all.'

She didn't look fine, however. I could see her chin wobbling slightly. Could a pleasant encounter, such as the one she'd just had with Amelie, *really* have upset her so much? There had certainly been no hint of that earlier. But perhaps she'd been keeping a brave face on some very pent-up emotions.

'It must have been a lot to take in,' I said, sipping my coffee. 'Finding out about your sister, and what had happened, and after such a long time.'

She nodded. Wiped her nose. Frowned. 'You could say that.'

'And you've also had a very long journey,' I suggested.

'I have,' she said. 'On all fronts. And *then* some. It's just been …' She seemed to be struggling to articulate something. I waited. 'It's just been …' she said again, '… just *so* overwhelming. And I can't seem to … sorry …' She brought the tissue to her face again. 'I am …

literally … I mean, *literally* overwhelmed … I'm sorry …' she mumbled, now from behind the tissue, and her shoulders began shaking, really shaking.

I had to quash my immediate instinct to go and physically comfort her – bloody Covid! – and instead could only use words. 'Oh, sweetheart,' I said, feeling suddenly, instinctively maternal myself. This woman was, after all, around the same age as my own daughter, and it was horrible to see her in such evident distress. 'I'm sure it has been. I can only imagine what you must be feeling. You must feel as if you have the whole weight of the world on your shoulders right now, and no one to help you carry it, either. I'll get some more tissues, and a glass of water. Just let it out, it's okay.'

I dashed back inside, grabbed the box of tissues from the coffee table, ran the tap and filled a glass with water. The rain had stopped now and rays of watery late-afternoon sunlight were beginning to inch their way across the grass.

When I returned, Robyn was still crying, though it seemed more a release now than an unstoppable compulsion. 'Here you go,' I said, placing water and tissues as near to her as the rules allowed. 'I can grab you a couple of paracetamol too, if you like. All that tension's probably going to give you a headache.'

She smiled wanly through her tears, then picked up the glass and drank. 'I'm okay,' she said. Then, putting it down, said, 'What's that thing about women and teabags?' She shook her head. 'I probably should have realised going to see her was a spectacularly bad idea.'

I was confused by the word 'going', as opposed to 'coming'. 'What, Amelie?'

'No, my sister.'

'You went to see your sister? What, before coming here?'

She nodded. And I wasn't really sure why I was surprised. She'd come all this way, after all. Why *wouldn't* she go and see her sister? Except with after everything I'd been told, well, it had just never crossed my mind. 'And it didn't go well, I'm guessing.'

'*Boy*, did it not go well,' she said, with feeling. 'You know how you tend to have this idea of yourself ... this idea that you can deal with anything that's thrown at you? I suppose we all do to an extent ... Because we need to believe we can fix things, don't we? Make things right?' I wasn't sure where this was going, but I nodded, because it definitely struck a chord with me. 'Well, this morning, I think I finally faced up to something I had never quite known I was still deluding myself about. You know? Specially since, you know, Mum died and everything, and I was so totally bound up in that. And I had completely lost touch with her by then, obviously.' She took another sip of water. 'I suppose I just buried it.'

'You mean fixing your sister?' I tried tentatively.

Robyn nodded a second time. And then the tears starting welling all over again in her eyes. 'You think you can, don't you? You always think that there's got to be *something* you can do. That you should do. Because that's what you *have* to do, right? Because you just feel so *guilty*.'

'I don't know you,' I said, 'so perhaps it's not for me to say, but from what you've told me, from what I *do* know, you have nothing to feel guilty about.'

'Guilt doesn't work like that, though, does it?' she said, brushing the tears from her eyes. 'And it's not even like I can blame him, is it?' she gulped another sob back. 'Much as I do. Because that makes *me* feel guilty *too*.'

'Him?' I asked.

'My *dad*.' She sighed a big, protracted sigh, then, to my surprise, jiggled her hands in the air, almost comedically. 'Hey, but that's the joy of suicide for you!'

The jaunty smile she'd affected disappeared again instantly, and another racking sob shook her shoulders.

'Your dad killed himself?' I asked gently. Another nod. 'When?'

'When I was 16, Kelly was 17.'

And Kelly, it turned out, had been the one who had found him. And, bit by bit, the jigsaw I'd only begun to piece together over the last couple of months began to come together, the full picture beginning to emerge from all the disjointed pieces. Like Kelly, their father had suffered with severe mental health problems. Chronic depression, in his case, which seemed to resist all interventions. He'd eventually hung himself one day, in the family home, and Kelly, arriving home from college that afternoon, had been the one to discover his body.

There had been no note, no nothing, just the appalling aftermath to deal with. Grief and shock, anger, their mother in bits. And though everyone agreed that Kelly's later mental health challenges might have been genetic, there was also no denying the effect her grim discovery that day had had on her. The spiral downwards was as swift as it had been severe.

'I think they call it survivor's guilt, don't they?' Robyn added, having composed herself a little now she was telling me the story. 'That it wasn't *me* that found him, that it wasn't *me* who'd inherited his cranky brain chemistry. That it wasn't *me* who'd basically imploded psychologically. I couldn't keep up with all Kelly's diagnoses, I really couldn't. Schizophrenia. Psychosis. Schizophrenia with psychosis. Bipolar. And we just felt so bloody powerless to do anything to help her, like we were watching it happening all over again. It felt like we were on suicide watch twenty-four seven. Till Amelie came along, anyway. And we really thought, Mum and me, well, at least we *hoped*, that having a baby to look after, well, that it might reset her in some way – that things might get better.'

Hopes that were clearly not to be fulfilled. 'When did your mum die?' I asked Robyn.

'About a month after I last saw Kelly.' She picked up the glass of water again and drained it. 'So that's one good thing, at least, to have come out of so much misery. She died before the worst of it. She didn't have to torture herself anymore.' She checked her watch. 'God, look at the time. I should go.'

I glanced at my own. Mike would hopefully still be out for another half hour or so. Robyn was calm again now, and she was no doubt exhausted, but I had this sense that she wasn't finished yet. I was also still anxious to know about her visit to her sister.

'There's no rush on my part,' I reassured her. 'Robyn, what happened today? With Kelly?'

She hooked her hair behind her ears. Sniffed, as if drawing a line under her tears and discomposure. Straightened herself to sit a little more upright in her seat. I could see her as a nurse somehow. Spit spot. Super-efficient. Kind but firm. Empathetic. 'You know, I thought I was prepared for a confrontation,' she said. 'I didn't want one, but I was ready. I mean, I know I'm not quite sure yet what I'm going to do about Amelie. It's such a massive commitment, after all, and I wanted – want – to be absolutely sure.'

'As you should be,' I agreed.

'So I needed to be sure from, you know, Kelly's position, that it really *is* true, that she really, *really*, no longer wants her, you know? That it's not just the illness.' I nodded my understanding. 'Because what if she *does* have a change of heart down the line? Even if the court says otherwise, I don't want that to deal with too. But I had no idea. I mean, *genuinely* no idea.'

'About what?'

'That she doesn't even believe Amelie is hers.' She shook her head. '*That's* where she's coming from. God, it's beyond any rationalising. I was actually there, at the birth. And the day after, and the day after. But that's where we're at. God knows what chemical chaos has been going on in her brain all this time. But she genuinely believes Amelie is not her child. That her real child was stolen – by the FBI, of course – and a different child put in her place.'

'A changeling,' I murmured.

'A changeling?'

'It's a word from myth. When a human baby was stolen by fairies, and a malevolent fairy put in their place.' I couldn't remember where I'd heard that, but it had just popped into my brain. It felt horribly appropriate.

'And she screamed at me. Properly screamed at me. Said I'd known all along. I thought it had just been the twins, but …' She spread her hands. 'Here we are. I have no idea how long she's had these feelings but it's clear, isn't it? I think she set that fire *knowing* it would kill them both. Even if she *did* change her mind – which she might – there's no knowing with such severe mental illness, is there? There is no way Amelie can go back to her. Ever. No one could – ever should – take that risk.'

I nodded, though she was staring above my head now, out at the clearing sky, as if the reality had only just crystallised in her mind. 'That's the basis on which we're proceeding now as well,' I said gently, 'as you've presumably already been told.'

Her gaze snapped back to me and `I sensed she had reached a decision. 'But to see her adopted. Spirited away to be brought up by strangers. How the hell, *in all conscience*, can I let *that* happen?'

# Chapter 19

I spent that weekend experiencing this weird sense of calm; a very different feeling to what had been my default for the entire time we'd been looking after Amelie – worrying what would happen, whether she'd move on without too much stress, where she'd end up, whether things would work out okay for her. No, I was now in full-on *que sera, sera* mode.

Once Robyn had left and we'd tucked a tired and happy Amelie up in bed, I had Mike order us a rare takeaway so I could bash out every bit of our conversation while it was all fresh in my mind. Because our conversation had galvanised me into this whole new mindset. And it wasn't just about the background to the current crisis, deeply tragic though all that was. It was because this virtual stranger, of whom I really knew so little, had looked and seemed so galvanised herself. And more than that, I had this powerful instinct that when she confirmed her decision – to proceed, or to walk away – it would be the right decision, either way.

Which was pretty weird conviction to have about someone I barely knew. But I trusted my instinct. Amelie would either make a life with her aunt (be it immediately or eventually), or she'd be adopted by loving strangers. And whichever of those outcomes transpired, I knew Robyn's decision would be made only after great deliberation. And that once made, it would never be revisited.

I don't know why I felt that so strongly – it was mostly intuition, nothing more – but I did. And by Monday night, a full day after I'd talked through everything with Christine, that intuition was confirmed, because Robyn sent me a lengthy email, having apparently already made it.

*So I recognised that I really had no choice to make*, she'd written, after running through the detail of the story sketched out in our conversation in the garden. *I have a small inheritance from Mum, so I'm solvent, so that's not an issue. And to walk away now would be to condemn myself to a lifetime of even more misery and guilt, and to not be able to look her memory in the face. To know my own flesh and blood is walking around somewhere, being looked after by other people – I might beat myself up – I do regularly! – but I'm not that much of a masochist.*

'That's a really good way of putting it, isn't it?' Christine said, when we chatted again on the Tuesday. 'And I really admire her honesty and self-awareness. To see someone so clear-eyed about their motivations is so rare and refreshing.'

'You're telling me! And I really do believe she'll make it work, too. She seems a very capable and level-headed young woman. So are the proverbial wheels about to be set in motion?'

'They are indeed. It might be a little while before it all comes together – complicated by the fact that she lives so far away, of course – but we're going to have a Teams meeting with her later this week. And I think she'd like to FaceTime with Amelie after that and see if she can sort things at work so she can make another visit. I thought it best that we get some things in place before putting anything to Amelie herself, so if you can keep her in a holding pattern till then, that would be great.'

'No worries there. She's got school to distract her for the next couple of weeks, and there's been very little discussed about the visit, to be honest. Only what a nice lady the nice lady was, and when's she coming again, and when she does, will she be bringing more presents …'

'Brilliant. So …'

'So? So *what*?'

'So now brace yourself, because I need to ask another favour.'

I laughed. 'Don't be coy, Chris. Of course we'll do another respite. I know we're due.'

'You say that now, but I haven't told you who yet.'

'Who then?'

'Katie and Jasmine. Could you bear having them back for another overnight later this week? I know, given how she behaved last time, that it's a bit of a big ask,' she went on. 'But we don't have anyone else with the room at the moment, and it's quite important.'

'Is she still with Sheila then?' I asked.

'Yes, for the time being. We're in a bit of stasis right now, to be honest. There's nowhere else we can put her, much less decide what's going to happen to them both longer term. Which means a bit of a stay of execution for her, really; she still maintains she wants to try and convince everyone to let her keep the baby and so far, she's been keeping her nose clean. Getting on better with the other mum, and not rocking the boat. Sheila's not convinced she can keep it up, but I guess time will tell. In the meantime we need a place for her for just the one night, while Sheila and her husband have some family business to attend to.'

I feared a funeral. Though the daily numbers of Covid deaths had dropped, you could hardly switch on the television without hearing about distressed, bereaved relatives who'd lost someone to the horrible disease. Thankfully, however, it wasn't that. Christine went on to explain that Sheila's elderly mum was in a nursing home some distance away, and, since she hadn't been able to see her for a long time, Sheila was desperate to go and visit, now the government had slightly relaxed the rules and were allowing window visits to care homes. Slots were obviously in high demand though, and needed to be pre-booked, and though they'd found someone to have the other mum and baby overnight, they had no one free to take Katie and little Jasmine. 'So, would you? You'd be doing Sheila such a huge favour. Which she promises she'll reciprocate down the line when she can.'

There was absolutely no question. It would obviously mean so much for her. And I knew someone else who'd enjoy a little baby time.

'Guess what?' I told Amelie, once Christine and I had made the arrangements for their arrival the following morning. 'Baby Jasmine's coming back for a night. Won't that be fun?'

Amelie clapped her hands together. 'Baby Jasmine!' she whooped excitedly. 'I've really missed her. Has she missed me?'

'Oh, I'm quite sure she has,' I said, 'And I'll bet she'll be full of smiles for you.'

'She loves me,' she said. 'You know how you're my second mummy? I'm like *her* second mummy, aren't I?'

What is it they say about things coming from the mouths of children? I didn't know it, but I was about to find out.

When Katie arrived the next morning, I could immediately sense a change in her. And though I fully accepted that that might be due more to wishful thinking on my part than cold hard reality, she wasn't slow in coming forward when it came to apologising for her behaviour during her previous stay with us.

'I mean it,' she said, once she'd brought in both baby and baby apparel, and we'd waved her weary-looking social worker off. 'I'm totally determined to do what's right for Jaz. I've been such an idiot, but I'm getting my act together now. Oh, hi, Amelie!' she trilled, as the beaming six-year-old came running in from the garden to meet them. 'Look at *you*!' she added, pretending to be astounded by what she saw in front of her. 'Is it me or have you grown a *whole inch* since I last saw you?'

'I'm nearly *seven*,' Amelie said proudly, by way of an answer. (It wasn't strictly true. As I recalled, her birthday wasn't till after Christmas. But, for Katie, it was, from me at least, a gold star sticker moment.) 'Can I help you change Jasmine's nappy?'

Katie folded her arms around Amelie for the requisite hug. 'Of course you can. I waited specially, just so you could. Do you want to help me with all my changing stuff?'

It really was like night and day. Unlike the last time, Katie seemed to genuinely want to engage with the family, to the extent that she barely seemed to glance at her phone, other than to record the duration and quantity of Jasmine's feeds in her app as she'd been shown to. Not that there was any worry on that front. Now more alert, and making eye contact – and, of course, repaying any attention she was paid with the most beautiful, dimpled smiles – Jasmine was looking decidedly bonny. Which made it all the harder to think that, even now,

Katie was still at great risk of losing her. I could only look on and pray she managed to keep it all up.

And, as expected, Amelie was constantly by her side, gently patting the baby, while Katie held her, to burp her, and beyond thrilled to be allowed to help her at bath time, and to hold her on her lap and – the biggest thrill of all – to give her her final bottle of the day.

'This has been the best day ever in my *whole entire life*,' she told Mike, when it was finally time for her story before heading to bed herself. 'When I grow up, I'm going to have a baby and I'm going to call it Jasmine. Jasmine means flower,' she added. 'Like the flowers in Katie's nanna's garden. That's why she's called Jasmine, I *love* her.'

Mike and I exchanged looks then. I knew he knew exactly what I was thinking. That there was, somewhere, a family, and a family that had once mattered to Katie, and presumably vice versa. Mattered enough to, knowingly or otherwise, bequeath a name to this new baby. I didn't know if Katie's nanna was alive or dead, or whether, if alive, she still saw her. Presumably not – the situation was probably multifactorial, challenging and highly complex. She and her baby were in care so we had to assume there was scant, if any, family to support her any more. That there had been no safety net to catch her and see her through. No Aunt Robyn to appear and save the day for her. It was just all so sad, and I almost had to forcibly push the thought process away, because going down that particular rabbit hole was so pointless.

# Little Girl Lost

After Amelie went to bed, it was time for Katie to settle Jasmine for the night. 'I'll go up too, I think,' she said. 'If that's alright? Catch up with some episodes of *Friends* on my tablet.'

It was still early. Not even gone seven yet. It was not long after midsummer's night, the hours of daylight still very long, and the sun was still streaming through the windows. But young mums of any age had long, tiring days, and, unlike last time, Katie had definitely done a lot of mothering today. Not least in entertaining Amelie as well. I felt a sudden, powerful ache for my own kids and grandkids. Still, we'd planned a big family FaceTime for the following afternoon, so at least I'd get to see them all virtually. 'Of course, love,' I said. 'You catch some shut-eye – you've still the night feed to get up for, after all.'

She shook her head. 'I've not had to do that. Not for the last week or so, anyway. She has a feed at 10 then she's zonked. She's slept through till seven twice this week already. Isn't that amazing?'

'Well, don't count those chickens. It's sometimes two steps forward then one step back with night feeds. But yes,' I agreed. 'A definite bonus. I remember having to feed our Riley through the night till she was almost a year old, so lucky you! You go on up, love. Take yourself a drink and snack up if you want to.'

'I'm good,' she said, and I smiled to myself, tickled by the way so many Americanisms had found their way into young people's language – not least, I suspected, from all that watching of old US sitcoms. And not just that – their viewing habits generally. Only the day before, I'd been chatting to Kieron and Lauren's eldest, my granddaughter, Dee Dee, and she told me that her little brother's 'garbage' truck had broken. And when we played shops, everything had to be paid for in dollars. Amazing how language constantly evolved.

I said as much to Mike once Katie and Jasmine had gone upstairs. 'Well, at least she's *been* good today,' he commented. 'It's been a good day full stop, really. Perhaps there's still a chance for her. In the meantime, how about we watch a movie?' He'd been scrolling through his phone. '*Outbreak*? *Contagion*? *The Andromeda Strain*? Ooh, how about this?' he said, showing me his phone screen. '*Quarantine*. That one sounds good, doesn't it?'

'What's this constant obsession with watching pandemic movies?' I said. 'You know, I'm seriously beginning to think you are losing the plot.'

'No, we're *living* the plot,' he pointed out. 'That's the whole *point*.'

'Go on, then,' I said. 'Though if anyone turns into a zombie, like the one we watched the other night, I. Am. Outta. Here. Okay?'

As it was, we both fell asleep about two-thirds of the way through, so we never did find out if anyone made it out alive. We ended up being woken up by the sound of Katie coming down again, to make up Jasmine's 10 o'clock feed.

'We're heading up now ourselves,' Mike said, stretching as he switched off the TV. 'Might as well make the most of an early night, eh?'

'Sleep tight, love,' I said. 'Hope she goes through for you.'

Though after that unscheduled powernap, I doubted I would. Still, I went to bed happy and, though I read for over an hour, I fell asleep feeling that familiar sense of quiet contentment, that it had indeed been a good day.

I woke up the next morning, however, feeling strange. I'd taken to not setting an alarm again for the past few nights, as the sounds of Amelie stirring would generally wake me, but I just had that sense that it was later than it should be. It felt too light, too hot, and I hadn't emerged from a dream. All evidence that I'd inadvertently slept in. I opened my eyes to see Mike was still fast asleep beside me, and when I turned to my left, it was to find that my bedside clock read 08:20.

Not ridiculously late, but why was the house in complete silence? Amelie was always awake around seven or not long after, and I knew from their previous stay – and because I knew babies generally – that a hungry baby Jasmine, billeted in the room next to ours, made enough noise to wake the dead. How on earth had I slept through all that?

I slipped out of bed and padded out to the landing in my nightie. Katie's bedroom door was closed and there was no sound coming from the room. Perhaps she'd had her morning feed and they were both asleep again. So I walked over to Amelie's room, the door of which was slightly ajar, as was normal, and as I approached, I could hear her chatting to her dolls and stuffed animals. Also normal.

'You're such a *good* girl,' I heard. 'Now let's see if this bot bot had got some orange juice in, shall we?' And as I pushed open the door, I anticipated the scene: Amelie in her current favourite *Finding Nemo* pyjamas, cross-legged on the floor, playing mummies. What I saw, though, had me open-mouthed in shock, because it wasn't a dolly Amelie was chattering to, it was Jasmine.

The baby lay gurgling on the carpet, in a very obviously soiled Babygro, while Amelie was trying to feed her from a plastic toy sippy cup.

She looked up as she saw me, her mouth forming a cheerful smile. 'I'm feeding baby Jasmine,' she told me. 'She's being such a good girl. *Aren't* you?' she cooed, looking lovingly towards the prostrate infant, who – thank goodness – looked none the worse for wear. Happy, in fact. Perhaps because there was an empty bottle on the carpet not far away from her. Not to mention the car baby seat she'd come with. But what the hell was going on? Had Katie dumped the baby in with Amelie so she could enjoy more of a lie-in?

'Don't pick her up, Amelie, okay? Do *not* pick Jasmine up. Just wait there a moment, okay?' I then hotfooted it back to Katie's room and flung open the door.

It was empty. As was the bathroom.

I went back into Amelie's room and scooped the baby up off the floor. I had no idea how long she'd been in there – some time, by the looks of things – but I couldn't risk Amelie taking it upon herself to pick her up and follow me. 'What's happened?' she asked, scrambling up as I headed back out and down the stairs, expecting to find Katie in the living room, doing whatever she might be doing, and fully intending to give her a piece of my mind.

But Katie wasn't downstairs either. With the sodden and soiled baby still in my arms, the wetness seeping into the fabric of my nightie, I pulled open the bifold doors and went to look in the garden, where the sun was already warm on my back. I went back in again, checked both the snug and the downstairs loo for good measure – the scene of so much carnage during her last visit to us. But she was nowhere to be seen; she was nowhere in the house.

Mike by now was heading down the stairs. 'Problems, love?' he asked, ruffling Amelie's hair. She'd toddled down after me and was now looking confused.

'Katie's gone,' I said. 'I can't find her.' I then turned to Amelie. 'Did she say anything to you, sweetie? When did she bring the baby in to you?'

Jasmine had begun grizzling now; she was clearly growing very uncomfortable. 'She didn't,' she said, as I bent down to slide the baby-changing mat out from underneath the sofa. We kept one there, along with wipes, cream and nappies, as my youngest grandson,

Carter, was still in them. Luckily, there were a couple of size-one nappies among them, which Katie had left down there yesterday. 'I just found her in her seat by my bed when I woke up. I thought you'd put her in with me, or Katie had, so I could feed her. Should I not have done?' she asked, getting down on her knees and opening the wipes while I started stripping off Jasmine's stinking Babygro and vest.

Mike had headed out front and now returned, scratching his head. 'No sign of her,' he said. Not that either of us had expected there to be. 'I'll head up to her room, see if she's left a note saying where she's gone.'

'She drank all her milk,' Amelie told me, passing me wipes, one by one, as I wiped the filth off Jasmine's bottom. Now she was stripped naked, and could feel the breeze on her, she was gurgling with pleasure, treating us to beaming smiles in that sweet, trusting way small babies did. She was too young to know her mother had apparently abandoned her. Her needs were being met and that was all that mattered. Separation anxiety didn't kick in till later. My own anxiety was on the rise though – where the hell had Katie gone?

'An' I was careful getting her out of her seat, like you showed me,' Amelie rattled on. 'I knowed to keep one hand behind her head all the time. Am I in trouble?' she then asked, already casting around in my little supplies basket to see if she could find a clean vest. I could have wept, bless her heart.

'Oh, no, sweetheart, not at *all*. You've been *such* a good girl. Baby Jasmine couldn't have been in more capable hands.' I reached across and stroked her hair. 'You really have been an angel.'

Mike reappeared then. 'No note. And no mobile, no charger, no handbag. I'm assuming you've tried calling her?'

I nodded. 'No joy.'

'So I'll call EDT, shall I?'

I nodded again. 'And put the kettle on, love? And can you fetch the play mat over, sweetie?' I asked Amelie. 'Let's get Jasmine set up there, and you can entertain her while we find out where her mummy's gone.'

Once Jasmine was enjoying the light show and bobbing characters and tinkling music (the play mat had been a bargain on eBay the previous summer), I dashed back upstairs for my own mobile, returning just as Mike was giving all the required information to the person on duty at EDT.

Though it felt as if I was personally sealing Katie's fate, I knew my next job was to call the police. She had, after all, effectively abandoned her baby. As with EDT, the protocols were time-consuming but straight-forward, and though I couldn't offer the sort of back-ground information I'd normally be able to – I knew the name Josh, but as far as I was concerned, Katie could be anywhere – they assured me they'd get what they needed from all the usual channels, and keep me posted on developments.

Finally, with a fresh mug of coffee in my hand, I telephoned Christine. 'I can't get my head around it,' I said, once I'd told her exactly what had happened. 'We had such a good day yesterday. She was like a different girl. I can't believe she was plotting to disappear the way she did, *or* that she'd come with an illicit bottle of vodka. And she must have sneaked out in the small hours, because I wasn't asleep till quite late.'

'It's a miracle the baby slept as long as she did,' Christine commented. 'But I agree. It sounds more like something happened. As in something perhaps happened with the boyfriend. I'd better call Sheila. She might have information that'll be useful to the police. In any event, she's going to have to pick up the baby. What time was she due with you?'

'Around one o'clock, I think.'

'Okay. So if Katie shows up in the meantime, let me know right away, won't you?' She paused before delivering the damning verdict I knew was coming. 'She won't be going back to Sheila's now, obviously. You'll have to make that clear to her.'

I looked across at where Amelie and Mike were on the floor, entertaining Jasmine. *Oh, Katie*, I thought. I really could have wept for her. Wherever she was, and whatever had made her do this, there would be no coming back from this now.

\* \* \*

It was a little after 11 when the police called us. A male constable who had the sort of world-weary air of someone coming to the end of a too-long and very tedious shift. 'We have her,' he said, adding 'safe and well', almost as if an afterthought. 'Her social worker is on his way to come and get her.'

'Has she said anything?' I asked. 'About where she'd gone or why she'd gone there?'

'Not a lot, to be honest,' he said, 'but she was with the boyfriend when we picked her up, and seemed a little worse for the wear. Vodka, I think she blamed. As they do …'

Twenty minutes later, we got a proper debrief from Christine. 'So she was actually picked up at the boyfriend's parents' house,' she explained, 'where they had pitched up around three in the morning.'

'What?' I said, astounded. 'And they said nothing? Did nothing?'

'Apparently they didn't know she was there until this morning. And reading between the lines, I suspect they're way past the point of having any control over their errant son. Officially errant, by the way. He's already known to the police, hence them being able to use the information Sheila was able to give them to track the pair down; they already had a few known addresses for him. He stole a car, by the way, so he could drive to yours and pick her up. Drove and met her in the next street so you wouldn't be alerted.'

'Oh, but why on earth did she go with him? What was she *thinking*?'

'They'd argued apparently. He didn't believe she was in respite. Thought she was off with some other boy – you know the kind of thing. According to Katie she'd only agreed to sneak out and meet him because he'd threatened to cause merry hell outside your house if she didn't. Thought she could placate him, I suppose.'

'But then to go off with him in the car! Why would she *do* that?' A thought occurred to me then. 'Before she left, she went to the trouble to make up a bottle, and left it by the baby when she'd snuck her into Amelie's room. So she must have expected to be gone for some time, mustn't she?'

'Evidently,' Christine said. 'But she was adamant that she never intended to be gone the whole night. Once he'd driven them all the way to his parents, though, there was little she could do. She was effectively stuck there, wasn't she?'

'She could have called us!' I sighed heavily. 'Why didn't she just call us?'

'Casey,' Christine said firmly, 'that particular horse has bolted and the stable door is closed now. I think it's easy to underestimate just what a hold this Josh character must have over her. She'd no more call you while she was with him around than fly in the air.'

'But it's all just so *frustrating*.'

'I know. But there's nothing we can do now. She'll be found a place to stay at an independent living hostel, and any contact going forward now will be supervised. You know the drill.'

I did indeed. Katie's actions would now set a sad chain of events in motion. Jasmine would go back to Sheila's as planned and if Katie wanted to fight to keep her baby – who would henceforth be officially in care – she would now have the fight of her life.

In the meantime, an hour later, Sheila arrived, and I felt really sorry for her as well. Though she would no longer have to worry about friction between the two young mums she'd been caring for, I knew she would feel, just as I did, so miserable about it all. You had to harden your heart, to an extent, in situations like this, and keep in mind that, for the baby, at least, a brighter future surely beckoned, because, in reality, perhaps Katie wasn't mature enough or strong enough to ensure her daughter the secure and happy life she deserved.

But that didn't make it feel any less wretched. And I struggled not to think about that young girl, no doubt full of remorse now, and where she might end up spending tonight, and the wretchedness and sadness that would be filling her head.

Despite trying our best to shield Amelie from the misery of the situation, she too could feel the weight of it pressing down, and said very little when Sheila arrived, except to ask if Jasmine could take one of her teddies with her.

'Oh, of *course*, poppet,' Sheila said, adopting the same upbeat, smiley visage as Mike and I were. 'She'd love that. That's really so kind of you.' So Amelie had chosen one of her teddies, and also one of her hearts and flowers drawings, and the farewell was as good as could be expected.

It was only as we watched Sheila unlock the car and strap the baby seat in that Amelie turned to me, her expression now grave and anxious. 'Why is that lady taking Jasmine away?' she wanted to know. 'She's not her mummy. Katie is Jasmine's mummy. Is she going to take her to Katie in her safe house?'

It was a question I didn't have the first clue how to truthfully answer.

'Yes,' I said, scooping her up and drinking in the scent of her freshly washed hair. 'That's *exactly* what she's doing.'

# Chapter 20

The situation with Katie hung like a heavy pall over the next couple of days. I'd been in similar situations with mother and baby placements myself, and I could all too easily imagine how the girl would be feeling now, as the reality of her future began sinking in. And however *laissez-faire* she'd been with Jasmine when she'd been with us – with *her* – I could imagine all too well how she'd be feeling right now. How she would be physically aching for her little baby. I also felt so bad for Sheila, who I knew would feel exactly the way I did – that once again all the optimism she had mustered had come to nothing (you had to feel optimistic about a young mother's chances, or you'd never ever go into that line of work), and, once again, all the nay-sayers had turned out to be correct.

The situation could easily provoke rage in me as well – what of the lad who'd got her pregnant? How was his future panning out? A night of fun … few consequences.

No, correction – *no* consequences. Would he – did he – even remember that passing bit of pleasure? But I made an effort not to go down that particular line of thinking; it served no purpose to get myself frothing with fury about the many inequalities in this world. Maybe one day, I'd switch jobs and get back into education; work in empowering young women, redressing the balance, making an unfair society a better, fairer, place. Right now, however, I had other things to be getting on with; the much happier business of doing all I could do to ensure Amelie's transition to a new life went smoothly.

There was no question that this was important time for Amelie. Life-changing in pretty much every sense of the word, and though it sometimes felt as if I was shoving Robyn down her throat on a daily basis, I knew it was important to keep her in the forefront of her mind, so that when the time came for her aunt to make the transition to her care, it was with as little anxiety as possible.

This wasn't just for Amelie's sake, either. While I felt as strongly as ever that Robyn was the kind of woman who would not backtrack on a commitment once she'd decided to take it on, there was a lot of distance to be travelled between 'doing the right thing' and feeling unconditional love for the child you'd committed to. Yes, they were closely related (both Amelie and Robyn took after Amelie's grandmother, Robyn had told me, whereas Kelly looked more like her father), but bonding between two people who barely knew each other couldn't be achieved via high hopes and the waving of a magic wand. It was something that happened gradually, increment by little increment, and I could have a useful role to play in that regard in the time Amelie remained with us, by making the process as stress-free as possible for her. This would, in turn (at least, so went my theory) mean Amelie was a joy to look after for Robyn, who would hopefully then find loving her all the easier than if Amelie felt anxious and unhappy in her care.

I would soon have a bit of time to help with that, too. Officially it was coming up to the summer break for school (which seemed ludicrous given that the children had barely been there for months), something else, having adjusted to going to school, that Amelie would also have to adapt to. So I was hoping I could bundle all the changes together and get a new Robyn-focussed future in place.

By the end of the penultimate week before the holidays, however, it seemed Amelie knew very well what was happening. On the way into school, I'd told her that this was the last weekend before school broke up and that she'd only be there for three days of the next, and was about to drop into the conversation that she'd be seeing Aunty Robyn on FaceTime straight after school, when she floored me.

'I know,' she said. 'You told me a hundred fifty thousand times already. And my teacher did too. We have the holidays and then we all go back to school in September, and me and my friends go into Terrapin class.'

Though, by now, of course, it was clear that she wouldn't be doing that, as she'd be enrolled in a school local to her aunt. I let that go, though, and instead concentrated on today. 'Well, you have a lovely day, and I'll see you this afternoon, and remember we've got a FaceTime with Aunty Robyn once you're home, so you can tell her all about it.'

Had she been a teenager, I suspect she'd have said 'whatever', but since she was a child, she just tugged her hand from mine and with a ''kay', was skipping off to join her 'bestest bestest friend', Bella.

I watched her go, and tried to remember that it was really very difficult for a little girl to form a bond with a virtual stranger who was little more than just a disembodied head and shoulders on a screen. We'd had three FaceTimes by now, and each time we 'met', I saw the poor woman's confidence falling further; Robyn was definitely less herself, I thought, when trying to make conversation in such an unnatural setting. I could see all too easily, even with the best preparation possible, that when the day came for her niece to go with her, permanently, that Amelie would be open-mouthed, maybe stunned even, with shock, and some terrible heart-wrenching scene would ensue. So I was tempted to suggest she and I have a FaceTime ourselves, just to reassure her that she didn't need to be so nervous around Amelie and to maybe suggest some ideas for things for them to discuss, which would help her over the uncomfortable pauses and times when I could just see Amelie was itching to get back to her painting, or her cartoons. Which wasn't unnatural; *all* children, particularly young ones, behaved similarly in those situations. Dee Dee, for instance, did not want to chat to Nanna for hours on end when she could be running around outside.

But this obviously felt more important. This was part of a process, not just a catch-up, and made harder by the fact that Robyn couldn't possibly know what made her niece tick, or the things she liked, and probably had no idea what the latest crazes among six-year-old girls were; you needed to keep your nose to the ground to keep up with all that stuff. And, by her own admission, bar her contact with Amelie when she was little, she had no experience with small children at all. But would I only make her more nervous if I suggested all this to her? More prone to worry and – whisper it – second thoughts?

While Amelie was in school that day I decided to give social worker Andy a call to run my thoughts by him. And he was definitely all for it.

'Well, I could say something to her if you like,' Andy said. 'And I know she's off work today because I was speaking to her an hour ago. But you know, it would definitely sound better coming from you. I feel that she might be a bit put off by a social worker saying we don't think she's being herself; she already feels uncomfortably under scrutiny, I think.'

I hadn't really thought a great deal about that, but the truth was that the cards were all in the authority's hands. It wasn't just a case of Robyn scooping Amelie up and skipping off into the sunset with her. As Amelie was legally the authority's responsibility, it would be up to them to agree to relinquish her into Robyn's care. And suppose my antennae were misfiring? Suppose there were things in Robyn's history that gave them cause to doubt she was a suitable person to become Amelie's legal guardian? What *then*?

So it was good to hear Andy reassure me. 'Which is silly,' he went on. 'She's been right through the mill, and we have no reservations about her at all. I guess it must be hard, though, feeling as if you're in a lengthy interview process to be allowed to claim the rights to your own niece.'

'But she's still as keen as she ever was?'

'Oh, absolutely,' he said. 'But she's frightened about everything moving so fast that Amelie will be deeply distressed about it all. She clearly loves the kid – she's spoken more than once about the times she spent with her as a baby and toddler – and she's emotionally intelligent enough to realise that the same won't immediately apply in reverse, specially now Amelie has bonded so well with you and your husband. So she's anxious about losing you both as a safety net.'

I had been in this situation several times before, particularly with children who'd been with us a while and were being moved on to people they barely knew

– be they carers *or* family members. 'But she won't,' I said. 'We'll be there for them as long as they need it. She does know that, doesn't she?'

'Oh, absolutely, it's just a question of deciding upon a strategy. Though, given the distances involved, and the fact that Amelie will need to be enrolled in a local school, I think it's safe to say that we don't have *that* much transition time, as a staggered move, doing weekends for a period and then gradually extending them, will be problematic, given the need to fit in with Robyn's work.'

'So this is all definitely happening? One hundred per cent? And sooner rather than later? And if so, when do we start priming Amelie herself?'

Andy laughed. 'Blimey, a few questions there!' he chuckled. 'So to break it down – I was going to pop all this in an email to you later today anyway, so don't worry about making notes – the court date is set for next week, and a judge will officially grant special guardianship to Robyn then, so we don't want to tell Amelie until that's done. Not that I'm afraid Robyn might pull out or anything, as I said. Like you, I think she's solid. But it *has* happened in the past, so let's not tempt fate, eh? And as for the actual transition, we think another visit, hopefully a sleepover, a little holiday if you like, with a moving-in date a couple of weeks later. And ideally not too far along in the school holidays. Her NHS trust have agreed special leave for Robyn during the summer break – which I believe is like being showered in gold dust – to give her time to settle in before starting at a new school.'

'Okay,' I said, 'wow, things really are motoring then, aren't they? And you know what? I don't think I'll say anything about Robyn seeming nervous. She's clearly not going to bottle out, is she? And it might just make her feel even more awkward. No, I think I'll just reassure her about how resilient Amelie is; I mean, look how she was the night she came to us?'

'Well, exactly,' Andy said, 'and, you know, don't think I'm telling you things you already know – I know you've been doing this way longer than I have – but we have to accept that it might be temporarily traumatic for Amelie to leave you even if we prepare the ground to the nth degree. That's just the nature of the beast, isn't it? We just have to remind ourselves that it will work itself out eventually. Believe that she'll settle in with her aunt just as she's settled in with you and Mike. Try and detach ourselves, just a *little*.'

I hear you,' I said, chuckling. 'You obviously have me taped, Andy! And no offence taken because I have to hear it from Mike *all* the time. It's the same with pretty much every child we care for. Though this time, I think Mike might need reminding as well – he's really become very attached to his little apprentice.'

'Was that my name I just heard taken in vain?' Mike asked, having come in just as we were reaching the end of the conversation.

'Oh,' he said, once I told him Andy's news, and how I

had realised how attached he'd become to Amelie. 'So she's leaving us that soon?'

I nodded. 'Seems like it. And I'm really happy. She's one lucky little girl. When you think about it, it's incredibly lucky that the news about the fire percolated through social media the way it did. It could equally have been that Robyn never saw it, and Amelie could have remained in care for ages. I mean, I know she's the sort of child who'd probably have no difficulty getting placed with an adoptive family, but we both know how long that whole process can take, so she might well have stayed in care for another two or three years.'

Mike nodded his agreement. 'Still, you know, I wouldn't have minded. You're not wrong, love. I really have grown very fond of her. I'm going to miss her when she goes.'

I could see he really meant it too. And I could see why, as well. This was the first time in all the years we'd been fostering that he'd not being going to work every day. The first time he'd been so involved in a foster child's life on a daily basis. No wonder he'd grown fond of her. They'd spent more hours together every day, in the space of a few months, than he'd ever had a chance to with his own children. I put my arms around him. 'So can I assume that when the time comes,' I ask him, 'you won't be sniggering at all my over-emotional snivelling?'

'I might be snivelling myself,' he admitted. 'Perish the thought.'

There was no time like the present, so, before walking down to pick Amelie up from school, I called Robyn.

'Oh, I know,' she exclaimed after I congratulated her on how far she'd come in the fostering process. 'It's been a bit of a whirlwind, to be honest. I had no idea it would all happen so quickly. And now I'm all flustered, of course, wondering how Amelie feels about it, trying to get her new room decorated, and, you know, I'm just not sure how ready *I* am. This is going to be one hell of a life-change.'

I laughed. 'You and me both,' I said. 'I think it's because it's a special guardianship thing rather than a fostering thing, it tends to be much quicker. Plus, the thinking is obviously to get her settled with you before school restarts in September. But yes, both Mike and me are a bit shell-shocked as well. We've both really grown very attached to her. But don't worry, I'm sure you'll have everything lovely for her. And to be honest, things like that matter less than you think. Though on that front, would you like me to write you a list of all her favourite things? That might help you feel you've created a space she'll feel at home in. Oh, and by the way, on that note, I've been told not to say anything to Amelie till after the hearing next week. I'm assuming you know that too?'

'I do. Andy told me earlier. Don't worry – I won't blurt anything out on FaceTime later. I don't want to terrify her. But we do need to make a plan for my coming to you for another visit, and us doing an overnighter somewhere – if she'll come with me, that is. I wish I could see her skipping off down the path with me, but I can't. Not yet, anyway. But I guess we'll just have to hope. Are there any dates you can't do?'

'I wish,' I said. 'Oh, how I'm pining for the holiday we're not going to be going on. But in reality, no. Whenever suits you. And I was thinking … re Amelie being reluctant to come away with you,' I said, 'just how friendly are you with the neighbour with the campervan?'

# Chapter 21

Due to the judge handling Amelie's case going down with Covid, it was actually the start of August before it was finally settled that Robyn was to legally become Amelie's guardian. And the very best news was that she'd not only stepped up: she was, assuming that was what was best for Amelie down the line, keen to adopt her as well.

It was all great news of course, but now we had to tell Amelie herself, something everyone felt a little nervous about, as we genuinely had no idea how well she would take it.

On the plus side, it had been a while now since Amelie had even mentioned her mother, much less expressed any interest in where she was or when she might see her. Yes, it was sad in one way – it would be nice to think she would retain some positive memories about her biological mother, after all – but, actually, it didn't really matter right now. The key thing was her bonding with her aunt. And that aunt obviously could and, I hoped, *would* re-introduce the memory of Kelly into their lives, just as she would her grandparents, and, much further down the line, share some of her sad story.

Since we'd laid the groundwork about Amelie not being able to live with her mother for the foreseeable future many weeks ago, I wasn't too worried about this. And so it proved; there was very little reaction from her at all. In fact, she was more interested in the prime minister's announcement that the lockdown was finally being lifted.

It seemed the whole country was rejoicing and, looking at all the images and clips, Amelie could feel the change of mood acutely.

'Is Christmas coming?' she asked on the morning of the announcement. 'Is everyone excited about Christmas?'

'No, darling,' I said, 'it's better than that!' (And, from me, that's saying something.) 'The prime minister has said we can all go out any time we like now, and we can meet up with friends and family. Aunty Donna's café can be opened again,' I added. 'We could all go down there for cakes and drinks soon, if you like. She does the most *amazing* homemade carrot cake.'

'Carrots in a cake?' Amelie said, pulling a face. 'That sounds ugh!'

'Oh, it isn't, you know. Just you wait and see.'

She was still disappointed, however, that it wasn't Christmas. 'So we won't be getting any presents then?

I member Christmas. Last Christmas, when I was still …
um … six as well, I think, I looked out for Santa for *hours*,
and he came, and I got' – she considered for a moment
then held a selection of fingers up to check – 'SIX
presents! Because Mummy said I was a *very* good girl.'

It was sad listening to her recount such a simple,
joy-filled memory. Had there at least been a modicum
of normality at that time of year? Perhaps there had. It
was also sad that I wouldn't be the one giving her a
magical Christmas *this* year – because I'd obviously have
gone all out to make it special for her.

'Oh, I love Christmas too, Amelie,' I said. 'I absolutely *love* it, and it won't be too long before it's here
again. I imagine your mummy will still look out for
Santa from her lovely new home, though, when the
time comes. What do you think?'

'Oh yes,' Amelie said, nodding. 'She'll be watching
because she always watches. Even with the tin foil on
the windows. But she won't need any presents because
she's a grown-up and grown-ups don't need presents.'

I had to say it then; I just had to test the waters.

'That's right,' I agreed. 'Well, at least not in the way
children do at Christmas. On Christmas Day, the thing
all the grown-ups love doing more than anything is
watching all the children open *their* presents. You know,
like Aunty Robyn loved watching you open the presents
she bought for you when she came to our house that
day, remember? And the one she sent you last week (she
had by now bought Amelie another dolly. She'd watched

Amelie open the box via FaceTime). And you know, maybe you might be at your Aunty Robyn's house for this Christmas,' I said, throwing it in as if I'd only just thought of it. 'Because she's your real family, isn't she? And oh, how lovely would that be? For you and your real-life aunty to spend Christmas together?'

Amelie seemed to digest this, but then simply shrugged. Now it wasn't actually Christmas yet, it was as if she no longer cared either way. 'Have we even had breakfast yet?' she asked. 'I'm starving!'

She had of course already eaten breakfast but she insisted she was hungry, so I made her a slice of toast and a cup of tea. In another small win – at least from the bonding point of view, it seemed that Amelie, like her aunt, enjoyed the devil's drink. I decided to try again.

'You know, Amelie, don't you, that your mummy will always be your mummy, even if you guys never live together? You get that, don't you?'

'Course I do,' Amelie said as she chewed her toast. 'Mummy got a sickness, like what that Andy told me, and Aunty Robyn told me, and she can't look after me, but that's okay cos I got you an' Mike to instead. So it's fine.' Another shrug of her shoulders.

'And your Aunty Robyn,' I reminded her, 'because she loves you *very* much. So of course she can look after you too.'

Now Amelie nodded, once again in that 'whatever' kind of way. Then said, 'Can I get down and go and play now?'

So clearly that was enough about the subject for Amelie, and I mentally noted that this was the first time in over a month that she'd shown any signs of her previous food issues. I would put it into my notes later that day and forward them to both Andy and Christine, and I felt comfortable that I had at least introduced the subject. Plus I knew, as mothers tend to, that the fact that she hadn't actually responded to what I'd said didn't mean she hadn't taken it in. At least I'd made an introduction to the idea of her living with her aunt, and she certainly didn't seem fazed about not living with her mother, so it was a promising start.

My next move was to arrange with Robyn to drive up and take Amelie off for their overnighter, as had been agreed before the court hearing. Ultimately it would make no difference now, because Amelie was going to live with Robyn, end of. But it would be *so* much easier when the day came, assuming it went well, if they had had that precious taster to help oil the wheels. And now that restrictions had been lifted it was so much easier to organise. Everything was opening up, and they could stay pretty much where they liked. But, of course, we all had other ideas.

'So, we're on,' Robyn said when we spoke later to arrange things. 'I've run everything by Andy and he has okayed it. I'm going to drive to you next Friday, and will hopefully be there late afternoon, and I've booked us into a great place just up from you on the coast. I'll bring her back to you Sunday teatime if that works for you?'

'That sounds fantastic,' I said. 'Oh, I can't wait to see her face. Oh, and I've accidentally on purpose left the relevant Peppa Pig episode on her tablet when she goes to the home screen. And it fits in nicely because today I started talking to Amelie about how nice it might be to live with you. I mean, it's early days, and I don't actually know that the hints sank in, but it's a start, isn't it? And I really do feel confident that a fun weekend away with you might just seal the deal.'

'Fingers crossed then,' Robyn said. 'And I was wondering … Do you think I might tell Amelie about it myself, on FaceTime?'

'You know what?' I said. 'I think it might be better over the phone? I think she's come to associate FaceTime with being in the spotlight and being made to sit still and be interrogated by grown-ups, whereas when the phone rings and she chats on it to someone, it makes her feel all grown-up and important herself. Shall I give her a shout? She's only outside with Mike.'

'Go on,' said Robyn. 'Let's do this.'

I could hear only one side of the conversation of course but it was at least reasonably edifying, consisting of lots of 'yes's and 'uh-huh's and even a couple of 'I didn't know we did that's. There was also a loud 'I LOVE fish and chips!' and an even louder 'Yay! You got presents!' (As I've said before, all methods *do* have a time and place.)

When she finally hung up and I looked at her enquiringly, Amelie simply beamed at me and said, 'I'm going

271

to the seaside with Aunty Robyn, and I need to pack my stuff in a shopping bag because she's already got me a Peppa Pig suitcase to put everything in.'

I only just managed to grab the phone she practically threw at me in her haste to return to the garden and tell Mike her exciting news. I followed her out. He was nodding and laughing. 'So can I assume that we're going to hear all about this every blinking minute till Friday now, kiddo?'

She held her palm up for a high-five. 'You betcha!'

The best, of course, was still yet to come. Mike had been right: Amelie had spent all the intervening time engrossed in making art, and not a single seaside motif was left out. And though I knew a couple of nights away did not a tearful and stress-filled final departure preclude, I had already made peace with myself about that. As Andy had said, it would be what it would be, and it would all come right before we collectively knew it.

In the meantime, however, I was simply excited. And come the Friday, Amelie didn't disappoint. She was stationed by the front window when Robyn pulled up, with her clothes and toiletries and favourite teddy in a supermarket bag for life, awaiting transfer to the promised Peppa Pig case. And when Robyn got out, case in hand, she clapped her hands together, then ran to the door to greet her, happy as a sandboy, even brandishing three 'very special aunty versions' of her heart paintings – special as in they all had robins on too.

They met halfway down the path and though Amelie didn't canon into Robyn with the same force and affection as she did Mike on a daily basis, she did hug her and their conversation seemed very animated. She then flew back down the path to where we were both just emerging with her stuff.

'Casey, you won't *believe* where we're going!' she told me breathlessly. 'We are going on a campervan holiday in Aunty Robyn's *campervan*! A proper campervan holiday, just like Peppa Pig does! And we're going to sleep in it, and wake up in it, just like they do! And we're even going to cook sausages, in a *field*! And guess what?' Her pretty eyes were now wide open in sheer delight. 'Aunty Robyn has a spotty dog, and he's called Rufus, and he's *actually in the van*. And he's coming on holiday with us too! I never had a dog. I'm SO excited!'

Robyn took the bag from me, her eyes shining. 'Booyah!' she mouthed silently. Then, 'Come on then, chick, we'd better get going, hadn't we?'

I could see the merest flicker of hesitation on Amelie's face now, but that fizz of excitement soon won out. And my hunch was that it was more about leaving us behind to miss the fun than concern about going away with her aunt. In that sense, I guessed, she was really no different to the little girl who'd pitched up at our house in the small hours almost four months earlier. 'Let's go then,' she said, smiling back at me and Mike. 'See you when I'm home again. Look after my other teddies for me.'

And with barely a backward glance, she was gone.

We waved them off and then stood on the steps for a few minutes. I had a lump in my throat and, as I looked at Mike, I could see he was barely holding it together too.

'For God's sake, love, she'll be back on Sunday,' I said, trying to make light of it. 'Bloody hell, if you're like this now, what are you going to be like when she goes for good in two weeks?'

'I'm fine,' he said gruffly. 'What are you on about, woman?'

'*It's* fine,' I said, warming to my theme now. 'Nothing wrong in feeling tearful. Don't worry, love, it doesn't mean you've gone soppy in your old age. It just means we've done a good job.'

I patted him and at last he dropped the facade. But it wasn't terribly long before he bounced back. It really didn't do for him to be letting his guard down so far. He had to do it all over again soon, after all. It was sweet, though, to see him feeling what I always felt. 'Speaking of jobs,' he said, 'Gary Marshall phoned me just before Robyn turned up.'

Gary Marshall was Mike's boss. 'And?' I said.

'And we're good to start back on Monday. Skeleton staff initially, but I'm one of them,' he said. 'At least, that's if I want to, no pressure.'

'And what did you tell him?' I asked as we headed back inside.

'Are you joking, Case?' he said, turning round and

gaping at me. 'I said I'd be there with bloody bells on. All very well, this full-time fostering, and I told him. I said I *needed* to get back. For the rest!'

# Epilogue

That weekend away was just what Amelie had needed to show her how much her Aunt Robyn loved her and wanted to take care of her. Rome was never going to be built in a day obviously, but it's amazing how quickly a child can feel emotionally secure with the right input from someone who loves them, and it was obvious that the two days the pair of them spent together would go on to form the first of hopefully thousands of memories Amelie would go on to carry through life. Indeed, not long after they returned it was Amelie herself who broached the subject of living with her aunt, casually throwing into conversation that she was going to go and stay with her for 'like, a long time, if that's okay?', as she put it. We obviously assured her that though we'd miss her, it was.

\* \* \*

When the day of the move came, a ridiculously far-too-quick nine days later, there were, as we'd expected, some tears. Again, not so much about going with Robyn, about which she seemed okay, but about leaving us, which was only to be expected. We'd co-existed so closely for quite some time now, after all.

'You know, it's not an either/or situation,' I explained to her. 'You can still come and see us. And Aunty Robyn can too. And we can speak on the phone and we can do lots of FaceTimes. In fact, I insist on it, because we're really going to miss you!'

And it *was* sad to see her leave the following Saturday. It all happened so fast we barely had time to digest it, and Mike and I *both* cried as we watched aunt and niece climb so cheerfully into the once again borrowed campervan. (I suspected Aunty Robyn might have to use that small inheritance to buy one …) Though, hilariously, our snivellings were truncated by a phone call. It was Amanda the psychologist, apologising for calling on a weekend, and for the ridiculously long delay, but she had some spaces the following week and could fit Amelie in – would we like to agree a date for her now?

Still, it was good to touch base with her, and to thank her for her input. She'd really concentrated my mind on the correct approach to take. 'And the proof seems to be in the pudding,' I quipped, as the campervan disappeared round the corner.

We all stayed in touch, of course, and for the first few months pretty regularly too. As well as chats with

Robyn, who made no secret of the fact that she was really grateful for all the support and advice we could give her, Amelie would video call us at least once a week, to fill us in on how she was doing, always full of excitement about absolutely everything, particularly when she started at her new school. We'd shake our heads sometimes in awe at just what Robyn had achieved with her. And were full of admiration for what she'd done for her niece. Her late mother, we knew, would be looking down and feeling such pride in her. We also hoped it would go some way towards reducing her entirely misplaced guilt. She was a lovely young woman, and we adored her.

As for Kelly, we never did hear any more about her. Her medical situation was obviously confidential, so why should we? Now we no longer looked after Amelie, it wasn't anything to do with us anymore. Though a part of me couldn't help stressing that she might come back into their lives and cause chaos once more. But as the months went by and no mention was made of her either by Amelie or Robyn, we knew the time for worrying, and also wondering, was over. Hers was an everyday tragedy, of the kind that breaks everyone's hearts but, in this case, at least one with a happy outcome for her daughter. We could only hope she was finding some peace from her distress and fear somewhere, and still getting the medical help she so badly needed.

Oh, and Robyn and Amelie *nearly* came and joined us that Christmas. With no real family of their own, it seemed a no-brainer to me and Mike, so we invited them both down to join the family for Boxing Day, and were all very much looking forward to it, too. But then, of course, that blasted virus got going all over again, and all too soon came that miserably familiar edict from the PM: 'You must stay at home …'

Oh, for pity's sake!

# CASEY WATSON

One woman determined to
make a difference.

Read Casey's poignant
memoirs and be inspired.

# I WANT MY DADDY

Five-year-old Ethan is brought to Casey in the middle of the night after the sudden death of his young mother from a drug overdose

When arrangements are made for Ethan to see his dad in prison, Casey recognises the name and face . . . It turns out she's far more familiar with this case than first imagined.

# I JUST WANT TO BE LOVED

Casey has fostered her share of vulnerable adolescents, but 14-year-old Elise brings unique challenges

When Elise makes some dark allegations against her mum, Casey doesn't know what to believe. Is Elise telling the truth? Casey is determined to find out and keep her safe.

# MUMMY, PLEASE DON'T LEAVE

When baby Tommy – born in prison – and his half-brother, Seth, are placed in the Watsons' care, their troubled teenage mother soon follows suit

Can Casey find the energy and strength to see this unusual case through?

## LET ME GO

Harley is an anxious teen who wants to end her own life, and there's only one woman who can find out why

Casey makes a breakthrough which sheds light on the disturbing truth – there is a man in Harley's life, a very dangerous man indeed.

## A DARK SECRET

A troubled nine-year-old with a violent streak, Sam's relentless bullying sees even his siblings beg not to be placed with him

When Casey delves into Sam's past she uncovers something far darker than she had imagined.

## A BOY WITHOUT HOPE

A history of abuse and neglect has left Miller destined for life's scrap heap

Miller's destructive behaviour will push Casey to her limits, but she is determined to help him overcome his demons and give him hope.

## NOWHERE TO GO

Eleven-year-old Tyler has stabbed his stepmother and has nowhere to go

With his birth mother dead and a father who doesn't want him, what can be done to stop his young life spiralling out of control?

## GROOMED

Keeley is urgently rehomed with Casey after accusing her foster father of abuse

It's Casey's job to keep Keeley safe, but can she protect this strong-willed teen from the dangers online?

## THE SILENT WITNESS

Bella's father is on a ventilator, fighting for his life, while her mother is currently on remand in prison, charged with his attempted murder

Bella is the only witness.

## RUNAWAY GIRL

Adrianna arrives on Casey's doorstep with no possessions, no English and no explanation

It will be a few weeks before Casey starts getting the shocking answers to her questions . . .

## MUMMY'S LITTLE SOLDIER

Leo isn't a bad lad, but his frequent absences from school mean he's on the brink of permanent exclusion

Leo is clearly hiding something, and Casey knows that if he is to have any kind of future, it's up to her to find out the truth.

## SKIN DEEP

Flip is being raised by her alcoholic mother, and comes to Casey after a fire at their home

Flip has Foetal Alcohol Syndrome (FAS), but it soon turns out that this is just the tip of the iceberg . . .

# A STOLEN CHILDHOOD

Kiara appears tired and distressed, and the school wants Casey to take her under her wing for a while

On the surface, everything points to a child who is upset that her parents have separated. The horrific truth, however, shocks Casey to the core.

# THE GIRL WITHOUT A VOICE

What is the secret behind Imogen's silence?

Discover the shocking and devastating past of a child with severe behavioural problems.

# A LAST KISS FOR MUMMY

A teenage mother and baby in need of a loving home

At 14 Emma is just a child herself – and one who's never been properly mothered.

## BREAKING THE SILENCE

Two boys with an unlikely bond

With Georgie and Jenson, Casey is facing her toughest test yet.

## MUMMY'S LITTLE HELPER

A young girl secretly caring for her mother

Abigail has been dealing with pressures no child should face. Casey has the difficult challenge of helping her to learn to let go.

## TOO HURT TO STAY

Branded 'vicious and evil', eight-year-old Spencer asks to be taken into care

Casey and her family are disgusted: kids aren't born evil. Despite the challenges Spencer brings, they are determined to help him find a loving home.

# LITTLE PRISONERS

Abused siblings who do not know
what it means to be loved

With new-found security and trust,
Casey helps Ashton and Olivia to
rebuild their lives.

# CRYING FOR HELP

A damaged girl haunted
by her past

Sophia pushes Casey to the limits,
threatening the safety of the whole
family. Can Casey make a
difference in time?

# THE BOY NO ONE
LOVED

Five-year-old Justin was
desperate and helpless

Six years after being taken into care,
Justin has had 20 failed placements. Casey
and her family are his last hope.

# TITLES AVAILABLE AS E-BOOK ONLY

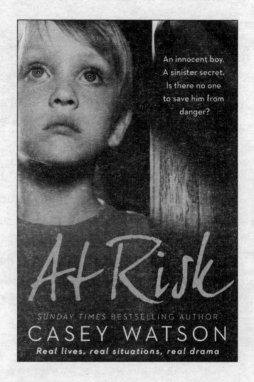

An innocent boy.
A sinister secret.
Is there no one
to save him from
danger?

*At Risk*

SUNDAY TIMES BESTSELLING AUTHOR
CASEY WATSON
*Real lives, real situations, real drama*

## AT RISK

Adam is brought to Casey while his mum
recovers in hospital – just for a few days

But a chance discovery reveals that Casey has stumbled upon
something altogether more sinister . . .

## THE LITTLE PRINCESS

Six-year-old Darby is naturally distressed at being removed from her parents just before Christmas

And when the shocking and sickening reason is revealed, a Happy New Year seems an impossible dream as well . . .

## DADDY'S BOY

Paulie, just five, is a boy out of control – or is he just misunderstood?

The plan for Paulie is simple: get him back home with his family. But perhaps 'home' isn't the best place for him . . .

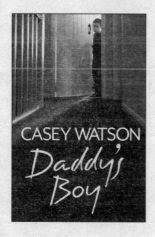

## THE WILD CHILD

Angry and hurting, eight-year-old Connor is from a broken home

As streetwise as they come, he's determined to cause trouble. But Casey is convinced there is a frightened child beneath the swagger.

## NO PLACE FOR NATHAN

Nathan has a sometime alter ego called Jenny, who is the only one who knows the secrets of his disturbed past

But where is Jenny when she is most needed?

## SCARLETT'S SECRET

Jade and Scarlett, 17-year-old twins, share a terrible secret

Can Casey help them come to terms with the truth and rediscover their sibling connection?

## JUST A BOY

Cameron is a sweet boy who seems happy in his own skin – making him rather different from most of the other children Casey has cared for

But what happens when Cameron disappears? Will Casey's worst fears be realised?

# FEEL HEART.
# FEEL HOPE.
# READ CASEY.

Discover more about Casey Watson.
Visit www.caseywatson.co.uk

Find Casey Watson on 🆓 & 🐦

# MOVING
*Memoirs*

Stories of hope, courage and
the power of love . . .

Sign up to the Moving Memoirs email and you'll
be the first to hear about new books, discounts,
and get sneak previews from your
favourite authors!

*Sign up at*

**www.moving-memoirs.com**